# 500
## salads

# 500

## salads

the only salad compendium you'll ever need

Susannah Blake

**SELLERS**
PUBLISHING

A Quintet Book

Published by Sellers Publishing, Inc.
161 John Roberts Road, South Portland, Maine 04106
For ordering information:
(800) 625-3386 Toll Free
(207) 772-6814 Fax
Visit our Web site: www.sellerspublishing.com
E-mail: rsp@rsvp.com

ISBN: 978-1-4162-0558-6
Library of Congress Control Number: 2009931643
QTT.FHSA

This book was conceived, designed, and produced by
Quintet Publishing Limited
6 Blundell Street
London N7 9BH
United Kingdom

Project Editor: Martha Burley
Editorial Assistant: Camilla Barton
Food Stylist: Liz Martin
Photographer: Michael Dannenberg
Designer: Tania Field
Art Director: Michael Charles
Managing Editor: Donna Gregory
Publisher: James Tavendale

10 9 8 7 6 5 4 3 2

Printed in China by 1010 Printing International Ltd.

Shutterstock images appear on pages 7, 11, 12, 15, 16, and 21.

Jacket image is Richardson, Alan/Stockfood America

# contents

# introduction

Salads are incredibly versatile and come in a seemingly endless array of colors, shapes, and sizes. Whether you're looking for a side dish or a filling main meal, a healthy snack, a wholesome lunch, a luxurious and indulgent treat smothered with creamy dressing, or a luscious fruity dessert, there's always a salad that's just perfect for you.

Most often thought of as a cold dish, salads can also be served warm—featuring fresh greens topped with hot or warm broiled poultry or fish, or perhaps tossed in a warm dressing just before serving. They can be light and leafy, consisting primarily of one of the many salad greens now available at most large supermarkets, or hearty and wholesome, based on cooked rice, pasta, or beans. Salads can be a meal-in-one—including meat, poultry, fish or shellfish, eggs, tofu, or another protein—or they can be an appetizer course, whetting the appetite for the meal to come.

Salads are perfect for almost any occasion. Sweet, fruity salads such as blueberry and papaya salad with toasted almonds (page 264) are wonderful for breakfast, brunch, or as a dessert, while a lighter salad such as watercress and apple salad with endive and bacon (page 53) can be a delicious choice for an appetizer. There are simple salads that appeal to children, such as two-tone coleslaw (page 177), and more sophisticated salads, like warm duck salad with honey–orange dressing (page 106). There are the classic salads of different cuisines, whether it's cucumber salad with yogurt and dill from Eastern Europe (page 41), tuna sashimi salad from Asia (page 246), Middle Eastern fattoush (page 25), insalata caprese from Italy (page 39), or cobb salad from the U.S. (page 32). And there are all those main-dish salads featuring a good balance of nutrients, vegetables, carbohydrates (such as pasta, rice, potatoes, or bread), and protein (such as chicken, meat, fish, shellfish, tofu, eggs, or cheese).

# equipment

Although you can make most salads using the most basic of kitchen equipment, there are a few essentials, plus a few handy extras, that will make salad-making easy.

### salad spinner
Salad leaves should be washed thoroughly to remove any dirt, grit, or other debris. It's drying the leaves that's tricky, because they're so easily crushed or damaged. Invest in a salad spinner, which will remove the water from the leaves, leaving them clean and dry and ready for use.

### chopping board
A basic chopping board comes in handy for slicing and chopping lettuces, vegetables, and fruit, as well as other ingredients such as broiled chicken breasts, cheese, and hard-boiled eggs.

### knives
A basic chef's knife is suitable for most salad-making needs. A serrated knife greatly simplifies slicing ingredients such as tomatoes.

### mandolines, slicers & graters
A mandoline will come in handy for recipes that require very thinly sliced ingredients, such as cucumber or carrots. A specially designed cheese slicer is useful for shaving off thin slices of cheese, but it also can be used to thinly slice cucumber. An egg slicer that allows you to

cut a hard-boiled egg into even slices in one motion can come in handy. Graters are great for shredding cucumber, carrots and other root vegetables such as beets, and cheese.

### vegetable peeler
Useful for peeling potatoes, carrots, and fruit such as apples and pears, a vegetable peeler can also be used to pare thin slices of carrot for salads, or shavings of Parmesan or Pecorino to scatter over the top.

### bowls & servers
Although many salads can be served individually, a large salad bowl is always invaluable—either for serving or for combining and tossing ingredients together. Smaller bowls can be used for mixing up salad dressings, and for holding prepared ingredients such as snipped herbs or sliced vegetables before combining and serving. Two large spoons are needed for tossing salads and serving.

### whisk or jar with screw-top lid
Although most dressings can be whisked together in a small bowl with a small whisk, it is even easier to put all your ingredients into a screw-top jar and shake together.

# ingredients

There's no limit to the type or quantity of ingredients you can put in a salad. You're likely to use lettuce or some type of salad greens, but even these aren't essential. Here are some ideas.

## salad greens

There are countless types of salad greens, all with their own distinct taste, texture, and appearance, and all providing a great base for salads. Some, such as iceberg or Romaine, are far more common than others, but look more closely at the produce section of your supermarket or shop at a farmer's market to find some of the more unusual varieties. Iceberg, green- or red-leaf lettuce, and baby spinach leaves will give you a mildly flavored salad, while nutty arugula leaves, peppery watercress, Belgian endive, escarole, and radicchio will add a distinctive, stronger flavor. A cellophane bag of mixed greens (often called mesclun) is ideal for many uses, providing different colored, shaped, and flavored leaves for maximum impact.

## vegetables

Lots of vegetables, raw or cooked, are great in salads. Not only do they add extra nutrients, they also add huge visual appeal with their various bright colors. Classic raw ingredients include cucumber, carrot, tomato, onion, bean sprouts, bell peppers, celery, and avocado. However, cooked ingredients—added warm or cold—can make a great addition too. Try roasted peppers, squash, red onions, and cherry tomatoes, cooked beets, or lightly blanched broccoli, cauliflower, and green beans. Cold cooked new potatoes are a great addition to salads and can help transform a light accompaniment into a main meal.

### fruits

Fresh fruits such as pear, apple, grapes, peaches or nectarines, kiwifruit, oranges, grapefruit, and berries can make a great addition to savory salads, providing a sweet, juicy tang. Fruits can also be used as the base of dessert salads and are delicious in most combinations. Select a few different fruits with different flavors, textures, and colors—such as apple, orange, and blueberry, or pineapple, mango, and strawberry—and simply peel or slice into bite-size pieces and toss with a splash of fruit juice or dessert wine.

### beans, pasta & grains

Adding hearty pasta, beans, or grains to a salad can be a great way of boosting nutrients and turning a light salad into a substantial one. All three provide plenty of healthy carbohydrates for energy, but beans contain lots of fiber and protein too. Whole grains such as brown rice and bulgur wheat are a good source of fiber, while some such as quinoa are a powerhouse of nutrients containing protein as well.

### proteins

Meat, poultry, fish, egg, cheese, and tofu are all delicious in savory salads. They are good combined with salad greens, pasta, grains, or beans and are made even more delicious with the addition of salad vegetables, fruits, and herbs.

# additions & embellishments

Adding little finishing touches to a salad, whether it's adding a handful of crunchy croûtons or a sprinkling of cheese, can transform a simple salad into something much more luxurious. Try some of these classic finishing touches.

### herbs
Fresh herbs can make a fabulous addition to both sweet and savory salads, adding both flavor and color. Fresh mint is particularly good in fruit salads, but it works well in savory salads too, for example in tabbouleh. Fragrant basil is especially well suited to tomatoes and Mediterranean-style salads, while fresh cilantro is a popular ingredient in Asian-style salads. Chives go well with egg, cheese, and potato-based salads, and dill is a classic flavoring for fish. Feel free to experiment according to taste, but be careful when using strongly flavored herbs such as rosemary, as their flavor can easily become overpowering.

### edible flowers
Many flowers are edible and make a stunning addition to salads. Most herb flowers are pretty and will add a lovely taste to salads, while other edible flowers include rose petals, nasturiums, lavender, violets, pansies, and zucchini flowers.

### croûtons
Crisp croûtons can add a delicious crunch to savory salads. Buy them ready-made from the supermarket or make your own. To make them, remove the crusts from thick-sliced white bread, cut the bread into cubes, then place on a baking sheet and drizzle with olive

oil (or a flavored oil such as garlic or chile oil). Toss the cubes to ensure they are evenly coated, then bake at 400°F for about 7 minutes until crisp and golden.

## cheese
All kinds of cheeses are good for embellishing a salad, but particularly good ones include Parmesan and Pecorino (either grated finely or cut into fine shavings using a vegetable peeler); crumbled blue cheese or feta, or strips of broiled halloumi.

## nuts
Nuts are a good source of protein and can add a delicious flavor and texture when sprinkled—either whole or roughly chopped—over a savory or sweet salad just before serving. Try toasting nuts such as pine nuts, peanuts, cashews, pistachios, and hazelnuts first. To toast, heat them in a dry frying pan, tossing over the heat for a few minutes, just until golden. Keep a close eye on them as they can easily burn, which will spoil their flavor.

## seeds
Like nuts, seeds are highly nutritious and can add a lovely crunch and flavor to salads. Pumpkin and sunflower seeds are great sprinkled over most savory salads, while tiny sesame and poppy seeds are good in grated carrot salads and coleslaw. Pumpkin, sunflower, and sesame seeds can be toasted the same way as nuts to bring out their flavor.

# dressing ingredients

Often adding a splash or drizzle of dressing is the final touch that transforms a salad from something good to something sensational. There are countless dressings from sweet and scented ones to sharp and tangy, rich and creamy, or spicy, light, or aromatic, but most start by combining a sharp liquid such as vinegar or lemon juice with an oil, plus other flavorings to enhance the combination. Choosing the vinegar and the oil for your salad is generally a matter of personal taste.

Olive oil, with its distinctively rich, fruity flavor, is a classic used in dressings. For the best results, choose extra-virgin olive oil obtained from the first olive pressing. For some salads, a good-quality olive oil can be used on its own as a dressing—for example, a simple tomato, mozzarella, and basil salad only needs a little seasoning and a drizzle of olive oil to be enjoyed at its best.

Oils such as canola, sunflower, and grapeseed have a much milder flavor and are great for dressings that carry stronger flavorings such as herbs, mustard, and honey, or even stronger Asian-style aromatics such as garlic, ginger, and chile pepper.

Balsamic vinegar is rich, dark, and sweet. It's great for making full-bodied dressings. The dark color of the dressing is often particularly good for drizzling and looks stunning over a fresh, brightly colored salad served on a white plate.

White and red wine vinegars, as well as sherry and cider vinegars, have a light, fresh flavor on their own and also combine well with other classic dressing flavorings such as mustard, honey, garlic, and herbs.

Fruit vinegars usually have a wine vinegar base so they have the same characteristics, but often with a fruity hint. Raspberry is a particularly popular fruit vinegar.

Lemon juice is one of the classic souring ingredients used for dressings. It has a light, very sharp flavor, so dressings made with lemon juice often benefit from the addition of a little sugar or honey.

# favorite dressings

There are hundreds of different dressings that are all delicious, and depending on which one you choose, you can transform the whole character of a salad. They can be light and zesty, rich and creamy, fresh and fruity, or tart and tangy. Those described below are absolute classics and are good drizzled over a simple leaf salad, as well as over more complex pasta, bean, grain, and vegetable salads.

### asian-style dressing
Stir together 2/3 cup rice wine vinegar, 2 tablespoons sugar, 1/2 seeded and finely chopped red chile pepper, and 1 tablespoon chopped fresh cilantro until the sugar has dissolved. Season with Thai fish sauce to taste. Alternatively, place the ingredients in a screw-top jar and shake together to combine.

### balsamic dressing
Whisk together 2 tablespoons balsamic vinegar, 4 tablespoons olive oil, and salt and freshly ground black pepper to taste. Alternatively, place the ingredients in a screw-top jar and shake together to combine.

### blue cheese dressing
Blend briefly in a food processor or blender 1/2 cup mayonnaise, 1/2 cup sour cream, 3 ounces crumbled blue cheese, 1 1/2 teaspoons white wine vinegar, and a good grinding of black pepper until smooth and creamy.

### caesar salad dressing

Whisk together 1/2 cup mayonnaise, 1 tablespoon Dijon mustard, 1 crushed anchovy fillet, 1/2 crushed garlic clove, 1 1/2 tablespoons olive oil, and 1/2 tablespoon white wine vinegar. Season with ground black pepper.

### honey-mustard dressing

Whisk together (or shake in a screw-top jar) 1 tablespoon Dijon mustard, 1 tablespoon honey, 1/2 crushed garlic clove, 2 tablespoons cider vinegar, 5 tablespoons canola oil, and a good grinding of black pepper.

### simple french dressing

Whisk together (or shake in a screw-top jar) 2 tablespoons white wine vinegar, a pinch of sugar, a pinch of salt, a good grinding of black pepper, and 5 tablespoons olive oil.

### sun-dried tomato dressing

Whisk (or shake) together 2 tablespoons red wine vinegar, 2 finely chopped sun-dried tomatoes in olive oil, a pinch of sugar, a pinch of salt, a good grinding of black pepper, and 5 tablespoons oil from the sun-dried tomato jar.

### thousand island dressing

Stir together 1/2 cup mayonnaise, 1 tablespoon ketchup, a good splash of Worcestershire sauce, 1 tablespoon minced parsley, 1 tablespoon snipped chives, and ground black pepper to taste.

# classic salads

There are so many salads to choose from, but it's

often the classics that you can't help picking, again

and again. This chapter brings the old favorites,

such as Caesar salad, chef's salad, and Greek salad,

right back into focus by adding a modern,

irresistible twist.

# fattoush

see variations page 42

Serve this classic Middle Eastern salad, made of chopped tomatoes, cucumber, and flatbread, for a light lunch or supper.

juice of 1/2–1 lemon
2–3 large, ripe tomatoes, in bite-size pieces
1/2 cucumber, diced
2 stalks fresh basil, roughly chopped
1/4 bunch fresh parsley, roughly chopped

for the toasted bread:
flatbread (approx. 14 oz.), such as pita bread
roughly 1/3 cup olive oil
sea salt and pepper

Mix the lemon juice with the tomatoes and cucumbers. Add the chopped herbs and toss to combine.

Dice the bread, put into a bowl, and sprinkle with olive oil. Mix well so that all the pieces are wet with oil. Put the bread on a baking sheet and toast in a preheated oven (325°F) for about 10 minutes, or until crisp and golden. Let the toasted bread cool slightly before mixing with the salad. Sprinkle with sea salt and pepper and serve.

*Serves 2*

# caesar salad

see variations page 43

Here's the ultimate recipe for a classic Caesar salad. Feel free to add your own personal touch to make a new classic recipe.

3 large cloves of crushed garlic
3/4 cup extra virgin olive oil
3 thick slices of stale white bread, crusts
    removed
2 medium-size heads romaine lettuce
salt and freshly ground black pepper

1 tsp. Worcestershire sauce
1/3 cup fresh lemon juice
2 tbsp. commercial mayonnaise
6 anchovies, drained and finely chopped
1/2 cup Parmesan, grated

Bruise the garlic with a heavy knife or rolling pin, and cover with olive oil. Marinate for 1 hour. Cut the bread into 3/4-inch cubes. Remove the garlic from the oil and set aside. Toss the bread cubes with 4 tablespoons of oil, and bake for 20 minutes at 300˚F, turning to toast evenly.

Remove the outer leaves of the lettuce. Tear the remaining leaves into 2-inch pieces and place in a salad bowl. Season with salt and pepper and toss with the remaining garlic-flavored oil. Mix together the Worcestershire sauce, lemon juice, and mayonnaise. Pour over the lettuce and toss. Add the croûtons and anchovies and toss again. Sprinkle with grated Parmesan and serve.

*Serves 6*

# frisée salad with blue cheese & bacon

see variations page 44

Salty bacon and tangy blue cheese are a classic combination—particularly in salads—and go together wonderfully here to create a light and flavorsome meal.

12 thin slices baguette
1 head frisée
4 bacon slices
1 cup (4 oz.) blue cheese, crumbled

for the dressing:
6 tbsp. olive oil
4 tbsp. sherry vinegar (or balsamic vinegar)
salt and freshly ground pepper

Toast the baguette slices under the broiler until golden brown on both sides.

Wash the frisée, spin dry, and tear into bite-size pieces. Arrange on plates. Cut the bacon into thirds and sauté in a dry nonstick skillet until crisp and brown. Remove and drain.

To make the dressing, whisk together the olive oil and sherry vinegar. Season with salt and pepper.

Scatter the cheese over the lettuce. Drizzle with dressing, scatter with bacon, and serve with the toasted baguette slices.

*Serves 4*

# potato salad with mayonnaise-yogurt dressing

see variations page 45

Potato salad, a favorite with everyone, is perfect for family meals, barbecues, and buffets. This version uses a tangy mayonnaise–yogurt dressing in place of the more classic mayonnaise.

2 1/4 lbs. firm-cooking white potatoes
2 scallions
for the dressing:
4 tbsp. white wine vinegar

3/4 cup mayonnaise
1/3–1/2 cup plain yogurt
salt and freshly ground pepper
chopped fresh chives, to garnish

Wash the potatoes and cook in boiling, salted water for 25–30 minutes. Drain, leave to steam dry, then peel and slice while still hot.

Wash and trim the scallions and cut into thin rings.

Mix the vinegar, mayonnaise, yogurt, salt, and pepper to make a dressing. Allow the potatoes to cool down slightly, then mix them with the dressing while they are still warm. Let the salad cool completely, stirring from time to time. Either stir the scallions in carefully or scatter over the top with the fresh chives before serving.

*Serves 4*

# cobb salad

see variations page 46

This great salad has a little bit of everything, making it a whole meal in a bowl. The first Cobb salad was created by Bob Cobb, manager of Hollywood's Brown Derby Restaurant in the 1920s or 1930s.

6 slices bacon
2 boneless, skinless chicken breasts
salt and freshly ground pepper
1 avocado
2 tbsp. lemon juice
1 small head lettuce (bibb or iceberg), torn
1 small head of radicchio, torn
1/2–3/4 cup canned corn kernels, drained
2 medium-size ripe tomatoes, sliced
2 hard-boiled eggs, sliced

1 red onion, cut into rings
2 tbsp. freshly chopped watercress, to garnish
for the dressing:
4 tbsp. oil
2 tbsp. white wine vinegar
1 tsp. strong mustard
2 tbsp. chicken stock
1 tsp. honey
salt and freshly ground pepper

Fry the bacon in a dry skillet until crisp and brown. Remove and drain on paper towel. Season the chicken breasts with salt and pepper. Fry on all sides in the bacon fat for 8–10 minutes, or until cooked through. Remove, drain, and let cool.

Peel and halve the avocado, remove the pit, and cut into wedges. Sprinkle with lemon juice.

Arrange the lettuce, radicchio, corn, tomatoes, eggs, avocado, and onion rings attractively on 4 plates. Mix the dressing ingredients, check the seasoning, and pour over the salad. Slice the chicken and add to the plate. Scatter with roughly crumbled bacon. Serve with watercress.

*Serves 4*

# chef's salad with thousand island dressing

see variations page 47

Everyone loves a hearty, wholesome chef's salad and this one, with its creamy and tangy thousand island dressing, certainly won't disappoint.

for the dressing:
1 gherkin
1 shallot
2 hard-boiled eggs
1/2 red bell pepper
scant 1/4 cup mayonnaise
3 tbsp. cream
3 tbsp. ketchup
salt to taste
chili powder to taste

2 boneless, skinless chicken breasts
1 head lettuce
6 oz. cooked ham
1 ripe tomato
4 hard-boiled eggs
3/4 cup grated Emmental or Swiss cheese
2 oz. Milano salami, sliced

To make the dressing, finely chop the gherkin. Peel and grate the shallot. Remove the yolks from the eggs (use the whites for another purpose) and push through a sieve. Put the bell pepper into a hot oven until the skin blisters, then pull off the skin and chop the pepper very finely. Mix the gherkin, shallot, yolks, and bell pepper with the mayonnaise, cream, and ketchup. Add salt and chili powder to taste. Pour the dressing into a small serving bowl.

Season the chicken breasts with salt and chili powder and cook in a steamer for about 8–10 minutes, or until done. Let cool, then cut into strips.

Divide the head of lettuce into leaves, wash, and spin dry. Cut the ham into strips. Quarter the tomatoes; remove the core, pulp, and seeds; and cut each quarter into 4 strips. Peel the hard-boiled eggs and cut into eighths. In a large bowl, toss the lettuce, ham, tomato, eggs, cheese, and sliced salami. Serve on individual salad plates and pass the dressing separately.

*Serves 4*

# apple & celery salad with walnuts & parmesan

see variations page 48

A twist on the classic Waldorf salad, this crisp, crunchy salad with sweet-tangy apple, wholesome walnuts, and a creamy, flavorsome dressing is hard to beat.

2 apples, thinly sliced
3 stalks celery, thinly sliced
1 fennel bulb, thinly sliced (use mandoline
    if available)
4 tbsp. chopped walnuts
1/2 cup freshly shaved Parmesan
for the dressing:
2 tbsp. mayonnaise

1 tbsp. cognac
1 tbsp. ketchup
scant 1/4 cup plain yogurt
2 tbsp. lemon juice
cayenne pepper, to taste
salt and freshly ground black pepper to taste
2 tbsp. nut oil (or canola oil)

Loosely mix the sliced apples, celery, and fennel in a large bowl, then arrange on 4 plates. Scatter walnuts and Parmesan shavings over each serving.

To make the dressing, mix the mayonnaise with the cognac, ketchup, yogurt, and lemon juice. Season to taste with salt and cayenne pepper. Drizzle the dressing over the salad and sprinkle with freshly ground pepper. Add a few drops of nut oil and serve immediately.

*Serves 4*

# insalata caprese

see variations page 49

An Italian classic, and perfect for serving as an appetizer, you'll never get bored with the fabulous combination of sweet red tomatoes, creamy white mozzarella, and fragrant green basil leaves.

2 tbsp. virgin olive oil
2 tbsp. lemon juice
salt and freshly ground pepper

2 medium-size ripe tomatoes, sliced
8 oz. mozzarella, sliced
small bunch fresh basil, to garnish

Mix the oil, lemon juice, salt, and pepper.

Arrange the tomato and mozzarella slices in a fan shape in small dishes and sprinkle with the dressing. Serve garnished with basil leaves.

*Serves 2*

# greek salad

see variations page 50

This classic salad is refreshing, tangy, and perfect for serving as an accompaniment at a barbecue, or as a meal-in-one with chunks of crusty baguette.

1/2 cucumber, peeled, seeded, and diced
1 green bell pepper, cut into strips
2 medium-size ripe tomatoes, diced
1 red onion, sliced into rings
1 romaine lettuce heart, torn in bite-size pieces
1 tbsp. black olives, pitted and halved
1 tbsp. green olives, pitted and halved
1 clove garlic, finely chopped
5 oz. feta cheese, diced

for the dressing:
4 tbsp. olive oil
2 tbsp. wine vinegar
1 tsp. capers
pinch of sugar
salt and freshly ground pepper
2 tbsp. chopped fresh basil, to garnish

Toss together the cucumber, pepper, tomatoes, onion, lettuce, olives, garlic, and cheese in a serving bowl.

To make the dressing, mix the olive oil with the vinegar, capers, sugar, salt, and pepper. Pour the dressing over the salad and toss to combine. Add more salt and pepper to taste, if desired. Carefully stir the chopped basil into the salad before serving.

*Serves 2*

# cucumber with yogurt & dill

see variations page 51

Variations of this classic cucumber and yogurt salad are enjoyed in numerous countries
countries including Turkey, Greece, Eastern Europe, and India.

1 large cucumber
1 small onion
2/3 cup low-fat plain yogurt

1/3–1/2 cup cream
salt and freshly ground pepper
fresh dill, torn into small pieces, to garnish

Peel the cucumber and slice lengthwise into long ribbons using a mandoline vegetable slicer
or a vegetable peeler. Pile loosely in 4 bowls. Put into the freezer for up to 30 minutes, until
just beginning to freeze.

Meanwhile, roughly chop the onion and put it into a blender or food processor with the
yogurt and cream. Blend until smooth. Season with salt and pepper.

Take the cucumber out of the freezer, pour the yogurt dressing on top, and serve garnished
with dill.

*Serves 4*

variations

# fattoush

see base recipe page 24

### fattoush with black olives
Prepare the basic recipe, adding 1/2 cup black olives to the tomatoes and cucumbers.

### hot & spicy fattoush
Prepare the basic recipe, stirring 1 teaspoon harissa into the lemon juice before combining with the tomatoes and cucumbers.

### fattoush with green pepper
Prepare the basic recipe, adding 1 seeded, diced green bell pepper to the tomatoes and cucumber.

### fattoush with fresh mint
Prepare the basic recipe, adding 1 1/2 tablespoons chopped fresh mint with the parsley.

variations

# caesar salad

see base recipe page 26

### chicken caesar salad
Prepare the basic recipe, adding 2 sliced broiled chicken breasts to the leaves and toss with the Parmesan and dressing.

### red hot caesar salad
Prepare the basic recipe, adding half a seeded and finely chopped red chile to the dressing.

### caesar salad with chicken and cashew nuts
Prepare the basic recipe, tossing 2 sliced broiled chicken breasts and a generous handful of toasted cashew nuts into the salad before tossing with the Parmesan and dressing.

### caesar salad with sweet chile tofu
Marinate 1 1/2 cups tofu (cut into 1/2-inch dice) in 1 1/2 tablespoons sweet chile sauce and 2 tablespoons soy sauce. Fry in a hot skillet with 1 tablespoon of oil until golden. Prepare the basic recipe and add to the salad and toss with the Parmesan and dressing.

variations

# frisée salad with blue cheese and bacon

see base recipe page 28

### frisée salad with feta cheese & cherry tomatoes
Prepare the basic recipe, replacing the blue cheese with the same quantity of crumbled feta cheese. Omit the bacon, and instead scatter 1/2 pound halved cherry tomatoes over the salad with the cheese.

### frisée salad with goat cheese & bacon
Prepare the basic recipe, replacing the blue cheese with the same quantity of diced goat cheese.

### spinach salad with blue cheese & bacon
Prepare the basic recipe, using 4 large handfuls of baby spinach leaves in place of the frisée.

### spinach salad with blue cheese & grapes
Prepare the basic recipe, using 4 large handfuls of baby spinach leaves in place of the frisée. Omit the bacon, and instead scatter 1/2 pound halved seedless grapes over the salad with the cheese.

### arugula salad with blue cheese & bacon
Prepare the basic recipe, using 4 large handfuls of arugula leaves in place of the frisée lettuce.

# potato salad with mayonnaise–yogurt dressing

see base recipe page 30

### potato salad with fragrant herb dressing
Prepare the basic recipe, adding 1 tablespoon each of snipped fresh chives, finely chopped fresh dill, and chopped fresh flat-leaf parsley to the dressing.

### potato salad with green olives
Prepare the basic recipe, adding 2/3 cup halved and pitted green olives to the potatoes before tossing with the dressing.

### potato salad with lemon dressing
Prepare the basic recipe, stirring the finely grated zest of 1 lemon into the dressing before tossing with the potatoes.

### potato salad with mustard dressing
Prepare the basic recipe, stirring 2 teaspoons wholegrain mustard into the dressing before tossing with the potatoes.

### potato salad with chopped egg
Prepare the basic recipe, sprinkling the salad with 1 chopped hard-boiled egg before serving.

variations

# cobb salad

see base recipe page 32

### vegetarian cobb salad
Prepare the basic recipe, omitting the chicken and bacon and add 4 sliced hard-boiled eggs instead of 2.

### cobb salad with seeds
Prepare the basic recipe, and sprinkle the salad with 1 tablespoon pumpkin seeds and 1 tablespoon sunflower seeds before serving.

### tuna cobb salad
Prepare the basic recipe, omitting the chicken and bacon. Instead, drain a 7-ounce can tuna, then flake the fish over the salad before dressing and sprinkling with watercress.

### mixed vegetable salad
Prepare the basic recipe, omitting the chicken, bacon, and egg.

variations

# chef's salad with thousand island dressing

see base recipe page 34

### swiss cheese salad with thousand island dressing
Prepare the basic recipe, omitting the chicken, ham, and salami.

### ham salad with thousand island dressing
Prepare the basic recipe, omitting the chicken, grated cheese, and salami.

### chicken salad with thousand island dressing
Prepare the basic recipe, omitting the ham, grated cheese, and salami.

### chef's salad with raspberry vinaigrette
Prepare the basic recipe, using raspberry vinaigrette dressing (page 63) in place of the thousand island dressing.

### chef's salad with honey–orange dressing
Prepare the basic recipe, using honey–orange dressing (page 106) in place of the thousand island dressing.

# apple & celery salad with walnuts & parmesan

see base recipe page 36

### apple & fennel salad with pecans & parmesan
Prepare the basic recipe, omitting the celery and using chopped pecans in place of the walnuts.

### apple & celery salad with hazelnuts & manchego
Prepare the basic recipe, using coarsely chopped hazelnuts in place of the walnuts, and shavings of manchego in place of the Parmesan.

### pear & celery salad with walnuts & parmesan
Prepare the basic recipe, using ripe but firm pears in place of the apples.

### arugula, apple & celery salad
Prepare the basic recipe. Place a handful of arugula leaves on each plate before topping with the salad.

### simple apple & celery salad
Prepare the basic recipe, using 6 celery stalks in place of the original celery and fennel. In place of the dressing, use 6 tablespoons mayonnaise.

variations

# insalata caprese

see base recipe page 38

### avocado, mozzarella & tomato salad
Prepare the basic recipe, adding 1 peeled, pitted, and sliced avocado to the tomato and mozzarella fan.

### mozzarella & tomato salad with balsamic dressing
Prepare the basic recipe, using 1 1/2 tablespoons balsamic vinegar in place of the lemon juice.

### insalata caprese with garlic toasts
Prepare the basic recipe. Broil 4 slices of ciabatta until golden. Cut a garlic clove in half and rub the cut side over the toasts, then drizzle with olive oil and serve with the salads.

### mozzarella & tomato salad with watercress
Prepare the basic recipe, omitting the basil. Instead, place a small handful of watercress leaves on each plate and arrange the salad on top.

variations

# greek salad

see base recipe page 40

### mediterranean olive salad
Prepare the basic recipe, omitting the feta cheese.

### tomato & feta salad
Prepare the basic recipe, omitting the cucumber and green pepper and using 4 tomatoes instead of 2.

### cucumber & feta salad
Prepare the basic recipe, using 1 whole cucumber in place of the half, and omitting the tomatoes.

### tomato & red onion salad
Prepare the basic recipe omitting the cucumber, and using 1 1/2 red onions and 4 tomatoes.

# cucumber with yogurt & dill

see base recipe page 41

### cucumber salad with yogurt & mint
Prepare the basic recipe, using 1 tablespoon chopped fresh mint in place of the dill.

### cucumber salad with yogurt & cilantro
Prepare the basic recipe, using 2 1/2 tablespoons chopped fresh cilantro in place of the dill.

### grated cucumber & yogurt salad
Prepare the basic recipe, but rather than freezing and slicing the peeled cucumber, grate it coarsely and let it drain in a colander for about 30 minutes.

### cucumber salad with cilantro
Prepare the basic recipe, replacing the onion with 6 sliced scallions.

# light & healthy salads

Crunchy fresh salad greens, zesty dressings, and

nutrient-packed ingredients such as nuts, seeds,

fish, and brightly colored fruits and vegetables

are brought together in these recipes to create a

fantastic choice of light and healthy salads.

# watercress & apple salad with endive & bacon

see variations page 77

The combination of slightly bitter greens with salty bacon, sharp apple, and sweet maple dressing is absolutely perfect in this light, tasty salad.

2 1/2 cups watercress
1 head Belgian endive, leaves separated
4 thick-cut bacon slices (or 5 regular slices)
1 apple, cored and cut into wedges

1 tbsp. pure maple syrup
3 tbsp. balsamic vinegar
4 tbsp. grapeseed oil (or canola oil)
salt and freshly ground pepper

Put a bed of watercress on each salad plate. Arrange the endive leaves attractively on the watercress.

Cut each slice of bacon into thirds, then fry in a dry skillet until crisp and brown. Remove bacon from the skillet and let drain on paper towel. Fry the apple wedges in the bacon grease on both sides until golden brown. Remove and drain on paper towel.

Mix the maple syrup with the balsamic vinegar and oil, then season to taste with salt and pepper. Sprinkle the dressing over the salad. Scatter the fried bacon and apple wedges on top and serve.

*Serves 4*

# organic bean sprout salad

see variations page 78

This simple, light, healthy salad is a great accompaniment to any meal. It makes a perfect choice to serve at a barbecue or with broiled meat or fish.

1 carrot
6 cups mixed organic bean sprouts
3 tbsp. apple cider vinegar

2 tbsp. nut oil (or canola oil)
salt

Peel and finely grate the carrot. Mix the carrot with the sprouts, vinegar, and oil and season to taste with salt.

*Serves 4*

# green salad with red cabbage & grapefruit

see variations page 79

Serve this light, refreshing salad with its bitter tang of grapefruit as an appetizer or an accompaniment to broiled fish or chicken.

2 grapefruits
1 tbsp. honey
3 tbsp. nut oil (or canola oil)
salt and freshly ground pepper
1 head oak-leaf lettuce, in bite-size pieces

1/4 head red cabbage, shredded
1 cucumber, halved lengthwise and sliced thin
2 tbsp. sunflower seeds
2 tbsp. pumpkin seeds

Finely grate the zest of 1 grapefruit. Then peel both grapefruit, remove the white pith and membrane, and cut out segments, avoiding the membrane. Work over a bowl to catch the juice. Squeeze the trimmings into the bowl.

Mix the grapefruit juice with the honey and nut oil, and season to taste with salt and pepper.

Arrange the lettuce, red cabbage, grapefruit pieces, and cucumber on serving plates. Scatter each serving with the seeds and grapefruit zest. Sprinkle the dressing over each plate and serve.

*Serves 4*

# mixed leaf salad with fennel & orange

see variations page 80

Fresh, sweet, zesty orange is the perfect partner for thinly sliced crisp fennel with its distinctive anise flavor. Serve this simple salad as an appetizer or accompaniment.

2 oranges
1 fennel bulb
for the dressing:
3 tbsp. sherry vinegar (or balsamic vinegar)
1 tsp. honey
1/2 tsp. hot mustard

3 tbsp. sunflower oil (or canola oil)
salt and freshly ground pepper
2/3 lb. mixed salad greens, torn in
   bite-size pieces
1 red onion, thinly sliced
fresh dill, to garnish

Peel the oranges and cut off the white pith using a sharp knife. Cut out the orange segments, collecting any orange juice in a small bowl. Squeeze the juice from the remaining pulp into the bowl. Wash and clean the fennel, quarter it, and remove the hard core. Shred the fennel into fine slices.

To make the dressing, add the vinegar, honey, and mustard to the orange juice and mix. Slowly drizzle in the oil and mix until it is well combined. Season with salt and pepper.

Arrange the salad greens, fennel slices, onion slices, and orange segments on salad plates. Drizzle each serving with the dressing. Serve garnished with dill.

*Serves 4*

# escarole & belgian endive salad with blood oranges

see variations page 81

Deep-red blood oranges help to create a stunning salad that's great for serving as an appetizer or accompaniment to broiled meat such as lamb kabobs.

1 small head escarole
1 head Belgian endive
2 blood oranges
1/2 cup plain yogurt
2 tbsp. crème fraîche

3 tbsp. apple cider vinegar
1 tbsp. honey
salt and freshly ground pepper
2 tbsp. capers

Wash and sort the escarole and Belgian endive, and coarsely shred the larger leaves. Arrange on individual salad plates.

Peel the blood oranges with a sharp knife, removing all the white pith. Cut out segments, avoiding the membrane. Catch any juice and squeeze the fruit trimmings. Mix the orange juice with the yogurt, crème fraîche, vinegar, and honey. Season to taste with salt and pepper.

Scatter the orange segments and capers over the escarole and Belgian endive. Drizzle with the dressing before serving.

*Serves 4*

# pear salad with walnuts & roquefort

see variations page 82

This light and refreshing pear salad, with its raspberry vinaigrette dressing, makes a wonderfully simple yet sophisticated salad for a dinner party or special meal.

1 bunch arugula
1 bunch watercress or garden cress
4–5 tbsp. roughly chopped walnuts
4 oz. (1/2 cup) Roquefort cheese, crumbled
2 ripe pears

for the vinaigrette:
1 clove garlic, finely chopped
6 tbsp. olive oil
4 tbsp. raspberry vinegar
1/2–1 tbsp. honey
salt and freshly ground pepper

Wash and dry the arugula and watercress and remove the stalks. Rip leaves into pieces and place in a serving bowl. Sprinkle with the chopped walnuts. Sprinkle half of the Roquefort into the bowl.

To make the vinaigrette, whisk the garlic with the olive oil and raspberry vinegar. Season to taste with honey, salt, and pepper. Pour the vinaigrette over the greens and mix well.

Peel the pears and remove the core. Quarter the pears or cut into slices. Put the pears in the bowl with the salad and toss gently. Arrange the salad on plates, sprinkle the remaining Roquefort over the top, and serve.

*Serves 4*

# spinach salad with strawberries & macadamia nuts

see variations page 83

Fresh berries are a great addition to leafy green salads, adding a distinctive sweet-sharp flavor and lovely juicy texture.

1 cucumber
2 1/2 cups fresh young spinach, washed
 and dried
2 cups quartered strawberries
3/4 cup shelled macadamia nuts
1 tbsp. whole-grain Dijon mustard

1 tbsp. honey
3 tbsp. white wine vinegar
3 tbsp. grapeseed oil (or canola oil)
salt and freshly ground pepper
1/2 bunch fresh chervil, to garnish

Peel the cucumber, halve lengthwise, scrape out the seeds, and dice the flesh. Put into a serving bowl with the spinach, strawberries, and macadamia nuts.

Mix the mustard with the honey, vinegar, and oil. Season to taste with salt and pepper. Add the dressing to the serving bowl and toss. Check the seasoning and serve scattered with chervil leaves.

*Serves 4*

# mixed vegetable salad with strawberries

see variations page 84

This simple vegetable and fruit salad is delicious served as an accompaniment to broiled fish, chicken, and meat. Make it in summer when strawberries are at their best.

1 tbsp. oil
1 tbsp. butter
1 small onion, very finely diced
1 clove garlic, very finely diced
4–6 tbsp. white balsamic vinegar
1 yellow bell pepper, cut in strips

1/2 cucumber
1 small head of lettuce, torn bite-size
1 1/2 cups quartered fresh strawberries
shredded fresh basil
fresh lemon balm leaves, to garnish

Heat the oil and butter in a small pan and sauté the onion and garlic until translucent. Stir in the vinegar and add the bell pepper. Let cool.

Thinly slice the cucumber, using a mandoline vegetable slicer if available. In a large bowl, mix the lettuce with the cucumber, strawberries, and basil. Add the onion and bell pepper dressing and toss to combine. Serve in bowls garnished with lemon balm.

*Serves 4*

# chopped tomato salad with scallions

see variations page 85

This simple salad makes a fabulous accompaniment to any meal, but it's also great piled up on slices of toasted baguette as bruschetta.

1/8 cup white wine vinegar
salt and white pepper
scant 1/4 cup olive oil

6 ripe plum tomatoes, diced
2 scallions, cut into rings

Mix the vinegar with salt and pepper and gradually whisk in the olive oil.

Mix the tomatoes with the scallions and put on plates. Drizzle with the dressing before serving. Serve with freshly baked bread.

*Serves 2*

# celery & orange salad with black olives

see variations page 86

Crisp, crunchy celery is a great addition to raw vegetable salads. Here, with sweet, tangy, juicy bits of orange, it's lovely.

4 cups sliced celery (or celeriac)
4 oranges
juice of 1/2 lemon
1/2 cup plain yogurt

2 tbsp. grapeseed oil (or canola oil)
salt and freshly ground pepper
1/4 cup chopped black olives, for serving

Blanch the celery in boiling, salted water for about 2 minutes. Refresh in cold water and drain.

Peel the oranges, removing all the white pith and membrane. Cut out the segments, avoiding the membrane. Dice the orange segments. Squeeze the fruit trimmings, then mix the orange juice with the lemon juice, yogurt, and oil. Season with salt and pepper as needed. Mix the orange pieces and celery with the dressing and put into glasses. Serve with chopped olives.

*Serves 4*

# endive & radicchio salad with mandarin oranges & seeds

see variations page 87

The combination of bitter salad leaves and sweet, juicy oranges is just divine in this simple but sophisticated salad.

1 1/3 cups torn lettuce leaves
1 small head radicchio, torn
2 heads Belgian endive, separated into
   individual leaves
2 mandarin oranges, divided into segments
1/2 cup halved seedless grapes

for the dressing:
4 tbsp. favorite vinegar
4 tbsp. favorite oil
1/2 tsp. honey
salt and freshly ground pepper
1 tbsp. each of peanuts, pumpkin seeds,
   and sunflower seeds

Put the lettuce, radicchio, endive, oranges, and grapes in a large bowl. Toss to combine.

To make the dressing, mix the vinegar with the oil, honey, salt, and pepper. Taste and adjust the seasoning as desired. Pour the dressing over the salad and toss. Serve the salad onto individual plates and scatter each serving with the nuts and seeds.

*Serves 4*

# green leaf salad
# with edible flowers

see variations page 88

Edible flowers make a stunning and delicious addition to salads. They are particularly suitable for meals for special occasions.

for the dressing:
3 tbsp. white wine vinegar
1 tsp. raspberry vinegar
1/2 tsp. mustard
pinch of sugar
salt and freshly ground pepper

for the salad:
5 tbsp. corn (or canola) oil
roughly 1 cup edible flowers (such as mallows, pansies, nasturtiums, carnations, borage, marigolds, or chrysanthemums)
3 cups mixed salad greens, torn in bite-size pieces

Mix the vinegars with the mustard, sugar, salt, and pepper. Whisk in the oil and set aside.

Wash the flowers if necessary, shake dry, and pat dry carefully.

Put the salad greens into a salad bowl. Add the dressing and toss well. Scatter the flowers over the salad and serve.

*Serves 4*

# salmon & vegetable salad in a cucumber cup

see variations page 89

These pretty, light, refreshing salads served wrapped in a slice of cucumber make a stunning appetizer for a special meal.

2 small cucumbers
salt
4–6 leaves green or red loose-leaf lettuce
1 apple, cut in 12 wedges
1 carrot, cut in long, thin sticks

1 pear, cut in long, thin sticks
1 avocado, cut into wedges
7 oz. smoked salmon
8 chives

Wash the cucumbers and peel 8 or so thin slices lengthwise from each one. Use the outer slices and the middles (the pieces with a lot of seeds) for another purpose (such as a salad). Lay 12 slices side by side and sprinkle with salt.

Wash the lettuce leaves and shake dry. Divide each leaf into 2–3 pieces, discarding the central vein. To make the cucumber rolls, lay a slice of cucumber on a work surface, top with an apple wedge, a few carrot and pear sticks, a slice of avocado, a little lettuce, and a slice of smoked salmon. Roll up. Tie with a chive. Stand the roll upright on a plate. Repeat with the other cucumber slices.

*Serves 4*

variations

# watercress & apple salad with endive & bacon

see base recipe page 53

### watercress & pear salad with endive and bacon
Prepare the basic recipe, using 1 pear in place of the apple. Peel and core the pear before slicing.

### watercress & apple salad with endive & sun-dried tomato
Prepare the basic recipe, omitting the bacon slices. Instead, thinly slice 5 sun-dried tomatoes in oil and sprinkle them over the salad before serving.

### watercress, apple & celery salad
Prepare the basic recipe, replacing the endive with 4 sliced celery stalks.

### watercress & apple salad with endive & walnuts
Prepare the basic recipe, omitting the bacon slices. Instead, scatter 1/4 cup walnut pieces over the salad before serving.

variations

# organic bean sprout salad

see base recipe page 54

### super-sprout & seed salad
Prepare the basic salad, adding 1 tablespoon each of pumpkin seeds, poppy seeds, and sesame seeds.

### spicy bean sprout salad
Prepare the basic recipe, whisking together the vinegar and oil with 1 tablespoon sweet chile sauce before tossing with the salad.

### gingery bean sprout salad
Prepare the basic recipe, whisking together the vinegar and oil with 1 teaspoon freshly grated ginger before tossing with the salad.

### bean sprout salad with blueberries
Prepare the basic recipe, tossing in 2/3 cup fresh blueberries with the bean sprouts and grated carrot.

### bean sprout & hazelnut salad
Prepare the basic recipe, sprinkling 3 tablespoons toasted chopped hazelnuts over the salad before serving.

# green salad with red cabbage & grapefruit

see base recipe page 56

### green salad with red cabbage & orange
Prepare the basic recipe, replacing the 2 grapefruit with 3 large oranges. Use the grated zest of 1 orange.

### green salad with grapefruit & avocado
Prepare the basic recipe, replacing the red cabbage with 2 handfuls of arugula leaves. Arrange the sliced flesh of 2 peeled, pitted avocados on the salad with the grapefruit and cucumber.

### green salad with red cabbage, grapefruit & parmesan
Prepare the basic salad, omitting the sunflower and pumpkin seeds and topping the salad with shavings from 1 ounce of fresh Parmesan.

### green salad with grapefruit, red cabbage & pistachios
Prepare the basic recipe, using 3 tablespoons chopped and toasted pistachio nuts in place of the sunflower and pumpkin seeds.

### green salad with red cabbage & apples
Prepare the basic recipe, using 3 sliced, cored apples in place of the grapefruit and 4 teaspoons white wine vinegar in the dressing in place of the grapefruit juice.

variations

# mixed leaf salad with fennel & orange

see base recipe page 58

### mixed leaf salad with fennel, orange & black olives
Prepare the basic recipe, scattering 2/3 cup pitted black olives over the salad before dressing.

### mixed leaf salad with fennel, orange & parsley
Prepare the basic recipe, sprinkling 3 tablespoons freshly chopped flat-leaf parsley over the salad in place of the dill.

### mixed leaf salad with fennel, orange & watercress
Prepare the basic recipe, using 4 large handfuls of watercress leaves in place of the mixed salad greens.

### mixed leaf salad with fennel, orange & scallions
Prepare the basic recipe, using 5 sliced scallions in place of the red onion.

### mixed leaf salad with fennel, orange & avocado
Prepare the basic recipe, adding 2 peeled, pitted, diced avocados to the salad plates.

# escarole & belgian endive salad with blood oranges

see base recipe page 60

### escarole, endive & orange salad with tiger prawns
Prepare the basic recipe, adding 9 1/2 ounces cooked and peeled tiger prawns (or jumbo shrimp) to the salad with the orange segments.

### escarole, endive & orange salad with artichokes
Prepare the basic salad, adding 6 jarred marinated artichoke hearts to the salad with the orange segments.

### escarole, endive & orange salad with poppy seeds
Prepare the basic recipe, sprinkling 2 tablespoons poppy seeds over the salad before serving.

### escarole, endive & orange salad with blueberries
Prepare the basic recipe, scattering 2 handfuls of fresh blueberries over the salad with the orange segments.

### escarole, endive & orange salad with chickpeas
Prepare the basic recipe, scattering 1 (15-ounce) can drained, rinsed chickpeas over the salad with the orange segments.

variations

# pear salad with walnuts & roquefort

see base recipe page 62

### baby spinach salad with pear & roquefort
Prepare the basic recipe, using 4 large handfuls of baby spinach leaves in place of the arugula and watercress.

### arugula, pear & parmesan salad
Prepare the basic recipe, replacing the watercress with an extra bunch of arugula, and the Roquefort with shavings of 1 ounce of Parmesan.

### pear salad with walnuts & parma ham
Prepare the basic recipe, using 6 strips of Parma ham, torn into bite-size pieces, in place of the Roquefort.

### nectarine salad with walnuts & roquefort
Prepare the basic recipe, using 3 pitted, sliced nectarines in place of the pears.

variations

# spinach salad with strawberries & macadamia nuts

see base recipe page 64

### spinach salad with raspberries & pistachios
Prepare the basic recipe, using raspberries in place of the strawberries and toasted shelled pistachio nuts in place of the macadamia nuts.

### spinach salad with peaches & pine nuts
Prepare the basic recipe, using 3 sliced, pitted peaches in place of the strawberries and 3 tablespoons toasted pine nuts in place of the macadamia nuts.

### arugula salad with strawberries & hazelnuts
Prepare the basic recipe, using arugula leaves in place of the spinach and 1/2 cup toasted hazelnuts in place of the macadamia nuts.

### watercress salad with strawberries & macadamia nuts
Prepare the basic recipe, using watercress leaves in place of the spinach.

### herb salad with strawberries & macadamia nuts
Prepare the basic recipe, omitting the chervil. Instead, add a small handful each of cilantro leaves, 2 tablespoons chopped fresh dill, and a small handful of fresh basil leaves.

variations

# mixed vegetable salad with strawberries

see base recipe page 66

### mixed vegetable salad with blueberries
Prepare the basic recipe, using blueberries in place of the strawberries.

### mixed vegetable salad with cherries
Prepare the basic recipe, using pitted cherries in place of the strawberries.

### mixed vegetable salad with raspberries
Prepare the basic recipe, using raspberries in place of the strawberries.

### mixed vegetable salad with kiwifruit
Prepare the basic recipe, using 4 peeled kiwifruits cut into bite-size pieces in place of the strawberries.

variations

# chopped tomato salad with scallions

see base recipe page 68

### chopped tomato & basil salad
Prepare the basic recipe, adding a small handful of torn basil leaves in place of the scallions.

### chopped tomato & mozzarella salad
Prepare the basic recipe, adding 1 mozzarella ball (about 1/4 pound), torn into bite-size pieces, with the tomatoes.

### chopped tomato & sweet pepper salad
Prepare the basic recipe, replacing the 6 tomatoes with 1 seeded and diced yellow pepper and 4 tomatoes.

### chopped tomato salad with balsamic vinegar
Prepare the basic recipe, using 2 tablespoons balsamic vinegar in place of the white wine vinegar.

### spicy chopped tomato salad
Prepare the basic recipe, whisking 1/2 seeded, finely chopped green chile pepper into the dressing.

variations

# celery & orange salad with black olives

see base recipe page 70

### celery & orange salad with walnuts
Prepare the basic recipe, using a handful of walnut pieces in place of the black olives.

### fennel & orange salad with black olives
Prepare the basic recipe, using 2 large, finely sliced fennel bulbs in place of the celery.

### celery & pear salad with black olives
Prepare the basic recipe, using 4 pears, cut into bite-size wedges, in place of the oranges, and stir 2 tablespoons orange juice into the dressing.

### celery & apple salad with black olives
Prepare the basic recipe, using 4 cored apples, cut into bite-size chunks, in place of the oranges and stir 2 tablespoons orange juice into the dressing.

### celery, orange & peach salad with black olives
Prepare the basic recipe, using 3 oranges and 2 peaches (pitted and cut into wedges) in place of the original 4 oranges. Stir 2 tablespoons orange juice into the dressing.

variations

# endive & radicchio salad with mandarin oranges & seeds

see base recipe page 72

### endive & radicchio salad with pears
Prepare the basic recipe, using 2 sliced pears in place of the oranges.

### endive, radicchio & orange salad with pecorino cheese
Prepare the basic recipe, omitting the nuts and seeds, and instead scattering shavings from 1 ounce Pecorino cheese over the finished salad.

### endive, radicchio & orange salad with poppy seeds
Prepare the basic recipe, using 1 tablespoon poppy seeds in place of the peanuts, pumpkin seeds, and sunflower seeds.

### endive & radicchio salad with plums
Prepare the basic recipe, replacing the oranges with 4 pitted plums cut into bite-size wedges.

### endive, beet & orange salad
Prepare the basic recipe, using 1 extra head of Belgian endive in place of the radicchio and adding 2 cooked (not in vinegar) sliced beets with the oranges.

# green leaf salad with edible flowers

see base recipe page 74

### green leaf & cucumber salad with edible flowers
Prepare the basic recipe, scattering 1/4 cucumber, thinly sliced, over the leaves with the flowers.

### green leaf & herb salad with edible flowers
Prepare the basic recipe, scattering 3 tablespoons chopped mixed herbs (such as parsley, chives, and mint) over the salad leaves before adding the flowers and dressing.

### green leaf salad with grapes & edible flowers
Prepare the basic recipe, scattering 1 cup halved seedless grapes over the salad with the flowers.

### green leaf salad with blueberries & edible flowers
Prepare the basic recipe, scattering 1 cup fresh blueberries over the salad with the flowers.

# salmon & vegetable salad in a cucumber cup

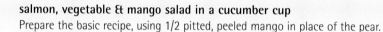

see base recipe page 76

### salmon, vegetable & mango salad in a cucumber cup
Prepare the basic recipe, using 1/2 pitted, peeled mango in place of the pear.

### salmon, vegetable & peach salad in a cucumber cup
Prepare the basic recipe, using 1 pitted peach in place of the pear.

### salmon, vegetable & dill salad in a cucumber cup
Prepare the basic recipe, sprinkling the carrot, apple, and pear with a little fresh dill before rolling up.

### salmon, vegetable & cilantro salad in a cucumber cup
Prepare the basic recipe, sprinkling the carrot, apple, and pear with 1/2 teaspoon chopped fresh cilantro before rolling up.

# warm salads

Simple salads made warm with the addition of
broiled meat, poultry, or fish, or perhaps a drizzle
of hot dressing offer a tantalizing twist to the
classic chilled or cool salad. They're great served
throughout the year—whether it's warm or
cool outside.

# warm lentil salad

see variations page 109

Firm lentils such as brown and Puy lentils make the ideal base for salads as they retain their shape once cooked. The salad is great served warm or cold.

2 1/2 cups brown lentils
1/4 cucumber
1 cup small cherry tomatoes, quartered
5 radishes, cut in small sticks
2 carrots, finely diced
2 scallions, finely chopped

1 red onion, finely diced
1 tbsp. finely chopped fresh parsley
for the dressing:
2 tbsp. safflower oil (or canola oil)
4 tbsp. apple cider vinegar

salt and freshly ground pepper
purslane (stems removed) and small salad leaves, to serve

Place the lentils in a large saucepan, cover with salted water, and bring to a boil. Turn heat to medium-low, cover, and simmer about 30–40 minutes or until tender. Drain well.

Peel the cucumber, halve lengthwise, scrape out the seeds, and finely dice the flesh. In a large bowl, mix the cucumber with the lentils, tomatoes, radishes, carrots, scallions, and onion. Add the chopped parsley.

Make a dressing from the safflower oil, vinegar, salt, and pepper. Pour the dressing over the lentil salad and mix well. Serve the salad on plates on a bed of purslane and lettuce leaves.

*Serves 4*

# warm goat cheese & spinach salad

see variations page 110

Spinach, bacon, and goat cheese are a classic combination. When the goat cheese is warm and melting, as it is here, it's especially delicious.

11 oz. goat cheese
4 slices baguette
8 slices bacon
1 tbsp. honey
juice of 1 lemon

3 tbsp. olive oil
2 tbsp. pine nuts
salt and freshly ground pepper
2 handfuls baby spinach

Slice the goat cheese into 4 equal slices. Toast the slices under a preheated broiler for 2–3 minutes, or until golden brown. Toast the baguette slices for about 1 minute per side, or until nicely browned. Fry the bacon in a skillet until crisp; drain on paper towels.

Meanwhile, mix the honey with the lemon juice, the olive oil, and the pine nuts. Season to taste with salt and pepper.

Put a bed of spinach on each plate, then add bacon and a slice of toasted baguette. Put the warm, toasted cheese on the baguette, sprinkle with dressing, and serve immediately.

*Serves 4*

# potato, chorizo & arugula salad

see variations page 111

Hot and spicy Spanish chorizo sausage gives a meaty bite to this warm fried potato salad. Serve as a light lunch or supper or a hearty appetizer.

2 potatoes
1/2 lb. chorizo, cut into slices
1 red onion, halved, thinly sliced
2 tbsp. balsamic vinegar
2 tbsp. olive oil

1 bunch arugula, tough stalks removed
salt and freshly ground pepper
1 pinch dried ground coriander
freshly grated Parmesan, to garnish

Peel the potatoes and cook for about 20 minutes in salted water until tender. Drain and let cool. Cut into quarters or eighths, depending on the size.

Sauté the chorizo in a hot pan, add the onion slices and potatoes, and continue to fry until golden brown. Remove from the heat.

Mix the balsamic vinegar and the olive oil together in a bowl. Add the arugula and season with salt and pepper. Now add the warm chorizo, potato, and onion mixture, and gently toss together. Season with coriander and arrange on plates. Serve with freshly grated Parmesan.

*Serves 2*

# cooked vegetable salad with basil

see variations page 112

Lightly cooked Mediterranean vegetables tossed with fresh basil leaves and served while still warm make a delicious meal accompaniment served with chunks of crusty bread.

1 1/2 lbs. fresh, ripe tomatoes, sliced
olive oil
salt and freshly ground pepper
1 carrot, peeled and sliced
14 oz. baby artichokes, trimmed and halved
4 cloves garlic, finely minced

1/2 lb. pearl onions, peeled
2/3 cup white wine
2/3 cup chicken stock
1/2 cup pitted, halved green olives
1 bunch fresh basil, roughly chopped

Put the tomatoes on a baking tray lined with waxed paper or parchment paper, and sprinkle with olive oil. Season with salt and pepper and broil under a preheated broiler for 1–2 minutes per side. Remove.

In a medium-size, ovenproof frying pan, heat a little olive oil. Sauté the carrot and artichokes. Add the garlic and onions, then stir in the white wine and stock. Cook until the carrot and artichokes are tender (or your desired firmness) and the liquid is almost evaporated. Stir in the olives, cook briefly to warm through. Brown quickly under the broiler, if you wish.

Put all the cooked vegetables into a salad bowl with the chopped basil and a little oil if necessary. Season to taste with salt and pepper and serve immediately.
*Serves 4*

# warm sweet potato salad

see variations page 113

Zesty ginger, spicy cayenne pepper, and fragrant cilantro are the perfect family for tender, buttery sweet potatoes in this simple, warming salad. The toasted macadamia nuts add a delightful crunch.

2 1/4 lbs. sweet potatoes, peeled and diced
1 1/2 cups macadamia nuts
2/3 cup vegetable stock
3 tbsp. white balsamic vinegar
3 tbsp. sunflower oil (or canola oil)

1 tbsp. honey
1 tsp. freshly grated ginger
salt and cayenne pepper to taste
1 bunch fresh cilantro

Cook the sweet potatoes in salted water for about 10 minutes, or until tender. Drain well.

Toast the nuts in a dry, nonstick skillet.

Mix the stock with the balsamic vinegar, oil, honey, and ginger. Add the potatoes and nuts and toss gently. Season with salt and cayenne pepper and let cool slightly. Pick off the cilantro leaves and mix into the salad. Check the seasoning and serve.

*Serves 4*

# eggplant salad with pomegranate seeds, herbs & feta

see variations page 114

Salty, crumbly feta and smoky, smooth eggplant make the perfect flavor combination in this Greek-inspired salad.

3 small-medium eggplant
5 tbsp. olive oil, plus more for brushing
salt and freshly ground pepper
1 pomegranate
juice of 2 lemons

1 clove garlic
sprigs of fresh parsley
sprigs of fresh mint
2/3 cup crumbled feta cheese

Wash the eggplants and cut into approximately 1/2-inch-thick slices. Sprinkle with salt and let stand for about 15 minutes. Then rinse with cold water and pat dry with paper towels. Brush the slices on both sides with some olive oil and season with salt and pepper. Broil on both sides under a hot broiler until golden brown.

Meanwhile, slice the pomegranate and carefully remove the seeds. Mix 5 tablespoons olive oil with the lemon juice. Press the garlic into the oil and lemon juice dressing and stir to combine. Sprinkle the warm eggplant slices with the dressing, toss, and let stand for 2-3 minutes. Pick the leaves from the parsley and mint sprigs and mix with the eggplant slices. Season to taste with salt and pepper. Put the eggplant salad on a platter, sprinkle with pomegranate seeds, scatter with crumbled feta cheese, and serve.

*Serves 4*

# marinated vegetable carpaccio

see variations page 115

Traditionally carpaccio is made of thinly sliced raw beef, veal, or tuna, marinated with garlic, olive oil, and other flavorings. Here, vegetables are marinated in a similar way to make a delicious salad that's perfect as an appetizer.

| | |
|---|---|
| 2 zucchini | 3 tbsp. white balsamic vinegar |
| 3 carrots | 1 tbsp. capers |
| 2 tbsp. sunflower oil (or canola oil) | 1 bunch fresh mint |
| 1 garlic clove, chopped | salt and freshly ground pepper |
| 2 tbsp. olive oil | dash of lemon juice |

Wash and trim the zucchini and slice thinly at an angle. Peel and thinly slice the carrots, also at an angle, using a mandoline vegetable slicer if available.

Heat the sunflower oil in a skillet and sauté the carrots and zucchini until golden brown. Add the garlic at the end. Remove and drain on a paper towel.

Put the vegetables into a bowl and mix with the olive oil, balsamic vinegar, and capers. Chop the mint (reserving a few leaves to garnish) and add to the vegetables. Season with salt and pepper, add lemon juice to taste, and leave at room temperature to marinate for at least 3 hours. Check the seasoning before serving.

*Serves 4*

# marinated leek salad

see variations page 116

This cold salad of tender, cooked leeks drenched in a zesty cilantro marinade makes a wonderful accompaniment to chicken or fish, or piled onto toast as a snack.

2 stalks celery, sliced
1 bunch cilantro, roughly chopped
1/3–1/2 cup grapeseed oil (or canola oil)
3 tbsp. balsamic vinegar

juice of 1/2 lemon
salt and freshly ground pepper
3 tbsp. olive or canola oil
4 leeks, in 3-inch lengths

In a medium mixing bowl, mix the sliced celery, chopped cilantro, grapeseed oil, balsamic vinegar, and lemon juice. Season with salt and pepper. Set aside.

Heat the oil in a large skillet. Add the leeks and slowly sauté over a low to medium heat until golden brown. Remove from heat and add to the celery–cilantro marinade. Toss to mix, then marinate for at least 3 hours. Season to taste before serving.

*Serves 4*

# arugula salad with sliced duck breast

see variations page 117

This elegant salad makes a wonderful appetizer for a special dinner party or a light supper or lunch served with chunks of crusty bread.

2 cloves garlic
1/4 tsp. cayenne pepper
6 tbsp. olive oil
2 boneless, skinless duck breasts (each
    weighing about 10 1/2 oz.)
salt and freshly ground pepper

for the dressing:
1/2 tsp. hot mustard
4 tbsp. balsamic vinegar
1–2 bunches fresh arugula
1 1/4 cups cherry tomatoes, cut into wedges,
    to serve
1 1/2 oz. wedge of Parmesan, to serve

Peel and press the garlic. Mix the garlic with the cayenne pepper and 2 tablespoons olive oil. Rub the duck breasts on all sides with this mixture, cover, and let stand for 1 hour.

Put the duck breasts skin-side down in a hot skillet and fry over a medium heat for about 8 minutes. Turn over and fry for 3 more minutes. Season with salt and pepper, wrap in aluminum foil, and put in the oven at 175°F for about 20 minutes to rest. Remove from the oven and let cool slightly.

Mix the mustard with the balsamic vinegar, salt, and pepper. Whisk in the rest of the oil and check the seasoning.

Wash and sort the arugula, spin dry, and arrange on 4 plates with the tomatoes. Sprinkle with the vinaigrette. Slice the duck breasts at an angle, then arrange the slices on top of the arugula. Shave the Parmesan with a vegetable peeler and scatter over the salad.

*Serves 4*

# warm duck salad with honey–orange dressing

see variations page 118

Duck and orange are a classic combination. This zesty honey–mustard dressing flavored with orange juice is wonderful drizzled over strips of pan-fried duck and nutty arugula leaves.

1–2 whole beets (about 1/3 lb.), depending
  on the size)
1/2 lb. arugula, tough stems removed
2 ripe mangos, peeled, pitted, and cubed
  (1/3-inch)
2 tbsp. freshly chopped chives
salt and freshly ground pepper
14 oz. boneless, skinless duck breasts
2 tbsp. oil
4 tbsp. freshly chopped parsley
2 tbsp. pumpkin seeds or sunflower seeds

for the dressing:
1/2 clove garlic, finely chopped
2 tbsp. freshly squeezed orange juice
1 1/2 tsp. Dijon mustard
1 tsp. honey
3/4 tsp. salt
1/2 cup olive oil
salt and freshly ground pepper

Wash the beet; remove the roots and the stalk. Wrap each beet in aluminium foil and cook in a preheated oven at 350°F for 1 hour until tender. Let cool, peel, and cut into 1/2-inch cubes.

Mix the garlic with the orange juice, mustard, honey, and salt. Slowly drizzle the olive oil into the dressing, stirring constantly, until it forms a creamy sauce. Season with salt and pepper. Mix 3 tablespoons of the dressing with the beet cubes.

For the salad, place the arugula in a bowl. Add two-thirds of the mango cubes. Add the chives and 5 tablespoons of the dressing and mix well. Season with salt and pepper and arrange on plates.

Cut the duck breasts into strips and season with salt and pepper. Heat the oil in a frying pan, add the duck strips, and fry until done to your preference. Remove the duck from the pan and mix with the parsley and 6 tablespoons dressing. Arrange the duck strips on top of the salads. Divide the marinated beet cubes and the remaining mango cubes over the salads. Garnish with pumpkin or sunflower seeds and serve.

*Serves 4*

# warm potato & egg salad

see variations page 119

This warm and colorful potato and egg salad is rich with the flavor of herbs and piquant shallot and makes a great choice for a buffet or barbecue.

| | | |
|---|---|---|
| 14 oz. firm-cooking potatoes | 1 tbsp. chopped fresh dill | 2 hard-boiled eggs, chopped |
| 1/2 cup vegetable stock | 1 tbsp. mayonnaise | salt and freshly ground |
| 1 shallot, finely diced | 3 tbsp. wine vinegar | pepper |
| 1/2 cup chopped radishes | 2 tbsp. sunflower oil (or | |
| 1 tbsp. snipped fresh chives | canola oil) | |

Wash the potatoes, then steam in their skins for about 30 minutes, or until cooked. Peel, let cool slightly, and slice.

In a saucepan, bring the vegetable stock to a boil. Add the diced shallot. Remove from the heat and pour over the potato slices. Mix in the radishes, herbs, mayonnaise, and vinegar. Finally, carefully stir in the oil and chopped eggs and season to taste with salt and pepper. Best served at room temperature.

*Serves 2*

variations

# warm lentil salad

see base recipe page 91

### warm lentil & spinach salad
Prepare the basic recipe, tossing 2 handfuls of baby spinach leaves into the lentils with the parsley.

### warm lentil & new potato salad
Prepare the basic recipe. Quarter 8 new potatoes and steam for about 10 minutes, or until tender. Add the potatoes to the salad with the tomatoes and other vegetables.

### warm lentil & herb salad
Prepare the basic recipe, replacing the tablespoon of parsley with 3 tablespoons roughly chopped fresh cilantro leaves and 2 tablespoons roughly chopped fresh parsley leaves.

### warm lentil & poached egg salad
Prepare the basic recipe. Poach 4 eggs in barely simmering water, then lift out of the water, drain on paper towel, and serve warm, one on top of each plate of salad.

### warm lentil & broccoli salad
Prepare the basic recipe. Divide 1/2 pound broccoli into florets and steam for about 4 minutes until just tender. Toss into the salad with the tomatoes and other vegetables.

# warm goat cheese & spinach salad

see base recipe page 92

### honeyed warm goat cheese & spinach salad
Prepare the basic recipe, drizzling each slice of cheese with 1 teaspoon honey before broiling.

### warm goat cheese & spinach salad with roasted peppers
Prepare the basic recipe, omitting the bacon. Instead, slice 4 roasted peppers (from a jar). Scatter the pieces over the spinach before adding the baguette and goat cheese.

### warm goat cheese, spinach & kiwifruit salad
Prepare the basic recipe, scattering bite-size pieces of 4 peeled kiwifruit over the salad with the bacon.

### warm goat cheese & spinach salad with pistachio nuts
Prepare the basic recipe, sprinkling 3 tablespoons roughly chopped toasted and shelled pistachios over the salad in place of the pine nuts.

# potato, chorizo & arugula salad

see base recipe page 94

### potato, chorizo & arugula salad with cherry tomatoes
Prepare the basic recipe, tossing a generous 1/2 cup halved cherry tomatoes into the salad with the fried chorizo, potatoes, and onion.

### spicy potato & arugula salad
Prepare the basic recipe, omitting the chorizo. Fry the onion and potato as before, but add a good pinch of crushed dried chile flakes.

### potato, chorizo & frisée salad
Prepare the basic recipe, using about half a head of frisée lettuce in place of the arugula.

### potato, chorizo & herb salad
Prepare the basic recipe, replacing the arugula and coriander with mixed salad leaves, 1 tablespoon snipped fresh chives, 1 tablespoon chopped fresh dill, and 2 tablespoons chopped fresh cilantro.

### potato, kabanos & arugula salad
Prepare the basic recipe, using Polish kabanos sausage in place of the chorizo.

# cooked vegetable salad with basil

see base recipe page 95

### cooked vegetable salad with basil & arugula
Prepare the basic recipe. Arrange a large handful of arugula on each serving plate, then spoon the salad on top to serve.

### cooked vegetable salad with basil & toasted pine nuts
Prepare the basic recipe, adding 4 tablespoons toasted pine nuts with the fresh basil leaves.

### cooked vegetable & couscous salad with basil
Prepare the basic recipe. Meanwhile, put 1 cup couscous in a bowl and stir in 1 tablespoon olive oil and a good pinch of salt. Cover with 1 cup boiling water and let stand for 5 minutes. Fluff up the couscous and toss with the cooked vegetables and fresh basil.

### cooked vegetable & fusilli salad with basil
Cook 1/2 pound fusilli in salted boiling water according to the package instructions, then drain and rinse in cold water. Prepare the basic recipe, then toss the pasta with the cooked vegetables and fresh basil leaves before serving.

variations

# warm sweet potato salad

see base recipe page 96

### warm sweet potato salad with basil & pumpkin seeds
Prepare the basic recipe, using a large handful of fresh basil in place of the cilantro. Omit the macadamia nuts and sprinkle the salad with 2 tablespoons pumpkin seeds before serving.

### warm sweet potato salad with mint & pine nuts
Prepare the basic recipe, replacing the cilantro with 2 tablespoons chopped fresh mint. Omit the macadamia nuts and sprinkle the salad with 2 tablespoons toasted pine nuts before serving.

### warm sweet potato & baby spinach salad
Prepare the basic recipe, tossing 2 large handfuls baby spinach leaves into the salad.

### warm sweet potato & roast pepper salad
Prepare the basic recipe, tossing 4 jarred roasted peppers, sliced, into the salad.

### warm sweet potato & beet salad
Prepare the basic recipe. Cut 7 ounces canned beets (not in vinegar) into bite-size chunks and toss into the salad.

# eggplant salad with pomegranate seeds, herbs & feta

see base recipe page 98

### zucchini salad with feta & pomegranate
Prepare the basic recipe, using 4 small-medium zucchini in place of the eggplant. (There is no need to salt the zucchini before cooking; simply slice, brush with oil, and broil.)

### eggplant, feta & basil salad
Prepare the basic recipe, omitting the pomegranate seeds. Toss a handful of torn fresh basil leaves with the eggplant in place of the parsley and mint sprigs.

### eggplant, herb & pomegranate salad
Prepare the basic recipe, omitting the feta cheese. Replace the parsley and mint springs with 2 tablespoons chopped fresh cilantro, 2 tablespoons chopped fresh flat-leaf parsley, and 1 tablespoon chopped fresh mint.

### eggplant, feta & sun-dried tomato salad
Prepare the basic recipe, omitting the pomegranate seeds. Instead, scatter 8 sun-dried tomatoes, drained and snipped into small bite-size pieces, over the salad with the feta cheese.

# marinated vegetable carpaccio

see base recipe page 100

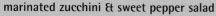

### marinated zucchini & sweet pepper salad
Prepare the basic recipe, using 2 seeded, thinly sliced red bell peppers in place of
the carrots.

### marinated zucchini & tomato salad
Prepare the basic recipe, omitting the carrots. Add 1 1/3 cups halved cherry
tomatoes to the sautéed zucchini before adding the marinade.

### marinated vegetable carpaccio with anchovies
Prepare the basic recipe, adding 4 anchovy fillets, which have been sliced into
long strips, to the sautéed vegetables before adding the marinade.

### marinated vegetable carpaccio with toasted hazelnuts
Prepare the basic recipe, sprinkling the salad with 3 tablespoons chopped toasted
hazelnuts just before serving.

### marinated vegetable carpaccio with fresh basil
Prepare the basic recipe, using 1 bunch of torn fresh basil leaves in place of
the mint.

variations

# marinated leek salad

see base recipe page 102

### marinated leek & sweet pepper salad
Prepare the basic recipe, sautéing 2 seeded red bell peppers, cut into large chunks, with the leeks.

### marinated leek salad with golden raisins
Prepare the basic recipe, adding 3 tablespoons golden raisins to the leeks with the marinade.

### leek salad with mixed herb marinade
Prepare the basic recipe, using 2 tablespoons freshly chopped flat-leaf parsley, 1 tablespoon chopped fresh dill, and 1 tablespoon chopped fresh mint in place of the cilantro.

### marinated leek & cherry tomato salad
Prepare the basic recipe, adding 1 cup halved cherry tomatoes to the leeks with the marinade.

# arugula salad with sliced duck breast

see base recipe page 104

### herb salad with sliced duck breast
Prepare the basic recipe, replacing the arugula with mixed salad leaves tossed
with a small handful each of fresh basil and cilantro leaves.

### arugula salad with duck & pomegranate
Prepare the basic recipe, scattering the seeds from half a pomegranate over the
salad just before serving.

### arugula salad with duck & blueberries
Prepare the basic recipe, scattering 1 cup fresh blueberries over the salad just
before serving.

### arugula salad with chicken
Prepare the basic recipe, using 2 boneless, skinless chicken breasts in place of the
duck. Do not pan-fry, but instead bake the marinated chicken at 425°F until just
cooked through.

variations

# warm duck salad with honey–orange dressing

see base recipe page 106

### warm duck & peach salad
Prepare the basic recipe, replacing the mangoes with 3 peeled, pitted peaches cut into bite-size wedges.

### warm duck & kiwifruit salad
Prepare the basic recipe, replacing the mangoes with 3 peeled kiwifruit, sliced into bite-size chunks.

### warm duck salad with artichoke hearts
Prepare the basic recipe, replacing the mangoes with 6 marinated artichoke hearts, cut into bite-size wedges.

### warm duck & pear salad
Prepare the basic recipe, replacing the mangoes with 3 peeled, cored pears, cut into bite-size wedges.

variations

# warm potato & egg salad

see base recipe page 108

### potato, egg & scallion salad
Prepare the basic salad, using 6 sliced scallions in place of the shallot.

### potato & chopped egg salad with capers
Prepare the basic recipe, adding 2 tablespoons roughly chopped capers to the
mayonnaise mixture.

### potato & quail's egg salad
Prepare the basic recipe, using 12 whole hard-boiled quail's eggs in place of the
chopped hard-boiled eggs.

### chopped egg & sweet potato salad
Prepare the basic recipe, using sweet potatoes in place of regular potatoes.

# grain & bean salads

Whole grains, beans, and lentils make a great base for salads—providing a healthy source of slow-release carbs for sustained energy, vegetarian protein, and essential fiber. They're wholesome, flavorful, and incredibly versatile—just perfect for making into exciting salad combinations.

# cilantro tabbouleh

see variations page 137

A Middle Eastern classic made with nutty bulgur wheat, lemony tabbouleh makes a wonderful accompaniment, particularly for broiled meats and fish.

1 1/4 cups vegetable stock
1 1/2 cups bulgur wheat
1 red onion, halved and thinly sliced
1 bunch fresh flat-leaf parsley, roughly chopped
1 bunch fresh cilantro, roughly chopped

2 1/2 cups diced, seeded tomatoes
3 tbsp. lemon juice
4 tbsp. olive oil
salt and freshly ground pepper

Heat the stock in a saucepan, stir in the bulgur wheat, turn off the burner, and let stand for 30 minutes. Then fluff up with a fork and let cool.

Mix the sliced onion, chopped herbs, and diced tomatoes with the lemon juice, olive oil, salt, and pepper. Then combine with the bulgur wheat. Season to taste and let stand for 20 minutes. Season again with salt and pepper before serving.

*Serves 4*

# quinoa with rosemary & bell peppers

see variations page 138

Highly nutritious and one of the only grains that constitute a whole protein, quinoa has been eaten for thousands of years. It was cultivated by the ancient Incas.

2 1/3 cups (14 oz.) quinoa
2 red bell peppers, diced
1 (14.5-oz.) can corn kernels, drained
2 scallions, sliced in thin rings
juice of 1/2 lemon
1 tsp. honey

3 tbsp. grapeseed oil (or canola oil)
2 tbsp. wine vinegar
2 tbsp. chopped fresh rosemary
1/2 tsp. dried coriander
1/2 tsp. fennel seeds
salt and freshly ground pepper

Cook the quinoa in salted water over low heat for about 15 minutes. Drain. Toss the quinoa with the diced bell pepper, sweet corn, scallion rings, lemon juice, honey, oil, vinegar, rosemary, coriander, and fennel seeds.

Taste, season with salt and pepper as needed. Chill for 30 minutes and check the seasoning before serving.

*Serves 4*

# warm chickpea salad with eggplant & zucchini

see variations page 139

This wholesome, nutritious salad makes a great vegetarian lunch or supper, but it is also fabulous with broiled meat or fish.

3 tbsp. canola or olive oil
1 small–medium eggplant, diced
2 small–medium zucchini, sliced
1 tsp. fennel seeds
1/3–1/2 cup vegetable stock

4 tbsp. soy sauce
1 (15-oz.) can chickpeas, washed and drained
1/4–1/2 cup pitted black olives
cayenne pepper
2 handfuls alfalfa sprouts

In a large skillet, heat the oil. Add the eggplant, zucchini, and fennel seeds, and sauté. Add the vegetable stock and soy sauce and cook for about 4 minutes. Stir in the chickpeas and olives and season to taste with cayenne pepper. Serve on a bed of alfalfa sprouts.

*Serves 4*

# rice salad with mozzarella & bell peppers

see variations page 140

When broiled, peppers become deliciously sweet, adding a luscious, juicy punch of taste and color to this simple rice salad.

2/3 cup rice
1 red bell pepper
1 yellow bell pepper
1 orange bell pepper
olive oil
salt and freshly ground pepper

1/4 cup pitted black olives
10 1/2 oz. mini-mozzarellas
1 bunch arugula, separated
3 tbsp. white balsamic vinegar
fresh basil leaves, to garnish

Steam the rice according to the package instructions. When done, remove from heat and let cool.

Wash and halve the bell peppers, remove the seeds and the white inner ribs, and roughly dice the flesh. Put on a sheet pan lined with waxed paper and drizzle with olive oil. Season with salt and pepper and put under a preheated broiler for about 4 minutes. Remove and let cool.

Put the cooked rice, peppers, olives, mozzarellas, and arugula into a serving bowl. Mix with 3 tablespoons oil and the balsamic vinegar. Season to taste with salt and pepper and garnish with fresh basil before serving.

*Serves 4*

# green bean & chickpea salad with cherry tomatoes & red onion

see variations page 141

This brightly colored salad is packed with healthy, nutritious ingredients and makes a great vegetarian lunch or supper, but is also good served as an accompaniment at a barbecue.

2 1/2 cups green beans
3/4 cup canned chickpeas, drained and rinsed
1 cup halved cherry tomatoes
for the dressing:
3 tbsp. white wine vinegar

4 tbsp. olive oil
salt and freshly ground pepper
3 tbsp. finely chopped fresh basil
1 red onion, diced

Wash, trim, and halve the green beans and cook in boiling, salted water until tender, about 6–10 minutes. Drain, refresh in cold water, and drain well. Put the beans, chickpeas, and tomatoes in a serving bowl.

To make the dressing, mix the vinegar with the olive oil, salt, and pepper. Stir in the basil and onion and check the seasoning. Mix with the beans, chickpeas, and tomatoes, and let stand for a while before serving.

*Serves 2*

# lenticchie all'umbra

see variations page 142

This simple rustic salad of lentils with tomatoes and pancetta has a wonderfully rich, earthy flavor. Add it to a summer meal, especially for al fresco dining.

2 tbsp. olive oil
2/3 cup finely diced pancetta
2–3 sprigs fresh sage, stalks removed
2 cloves garlic, finely chopped
2–3 sprigs of fresh thyme
2 cups brown or greenish lentils
    (presoaked according to
    package instructions)

1 1/2 cups stock
1 cup red wine
3 cups peeled, seeded, and diced tomatoes
salt and freshly ground pepper
white wine vinegar
fresh basil leaves, to garnish

Heat the oil in a deep skillet and fry the pancetta until crisp. Remove about a third of the pancetta and set aside. Finely chop the sage leaves. Add the garlic, herbs, and lentils to the skillet and sauté briefly. Add the stock and red wine and simmer over moderate heat for around 10–15 minutes.

Add the diced tomatoes to the skillet, mix, and cook for another 10 minutes or so. Season with salt and pepper and add a little vinegar to taste. Serve sprinkled with the basil and the reserved pancetta.

*Serves 4–6*

# wild rice salad with walnuts & dried cranberries

see variations page 143

Wild rice has long, slim grains and a nuttier, firmer texture than regular rice. This salad, with its nuts, dried cranberries, herbs, and spicy dressing, makes a great side dish.

1 cup wild rice
3/4 cup chopped walnuts
2 tbsp. chopped fresh mint
1/3 cup dried cranberries

juice of 1 lemon
2 tbsp. peanut oil (or canola oil)
salt and cayenne pepper

Cook the rice in boiling, salted water for about 40 minutes, or until done. Drain and let cool. Mix the rice with the rest of the ingredients and season to taste with salt and cayenne pepper.

*Serves 4*

# green bean salad with sesame & cilantro

see variations page 144

Fresh, sweet green beans are one of the joys of summer. Try this simple green bean salad spiked with Asian flavors at your next cookout.

1 1/4–1 1/2 lbs. green beans
1 tbsp. butter
1 clove garlic, finely chopped
1/2-inch piece of fresh ginger, peeled
    and finely diced
2 tbsp. peanut oil (or canola oil)

3–4 tbsp. dark soy sauce
1–2 tbsp. rice vinegar
2 tbsp. sesame seeds
salt and pepper
pinch of sugar
1 tsp. finely chopped cilantro, to serve

Wash, top, and tail the beans, and halve if necessary. Blanch in plenty of boiling, salted water until tender, about 6–10 minutes. Drain and refresh in ice-cold water.

Heat the butter in a skillet, add the garlic and ginger, and sauté, stirring. Add the peanut oil and the beans. Stir in the soy sauce, rice vinegar, and sesame seeds. Season with salt, pepper, and a pinch of sugar. Sprinkle with cilantro. Serve in bowls, warm or cold.

*Serves 4*

# bean salad with red onions & parsley

see variations page 145

A simple bean salad makes a great addition to a barbecue or buffet, but is also a delicious accompaniment to serve with kabobs and other broiled meats.

2 cups canned flageolet beans in water
3 tbsp. extra-virgin olive oil
2 red onions, finely chopped

salt and freshly ground pepper
2–3 tbsp. white wine vinegar or to taste
1 bunch fresh parsley, chopped

Drain the beans and gently rinse. Mix the beans with the oil and chopped onions. Season with salt and pepper and add vinegar to taste. Mix in the parsley, check the seasonings, and serve.

*Serves 4*

# cilantro tabbouleh

see base recipe page 121

### cilantro tabbouleh with smoked trout
Prepare the basic recipe, adding 2 flaked smoked trout fillets with the chopped herbs and tomatoes.

### cilantro tabbouleh with poached eggs
Prepare the basic recipe. To serve, poach 4 eggs in boiling water for about 4 minutes, then lift out and pat dry on paper towels. Spoon the tabbouleh into 4 bowls and top each serving with a poached egg.

### cilantro tabbouleh with ham
Prepare the basic recipe, adding 7 oz. ham cut into strips with the chopped herbs and tomatoes.

### cilantro tabbouleh with chickpeas
Prepare the basic recipe, adding 1 2/3 cups canned chickpeas (drained and rinsed) with the chopped herbs and tomatoes.

### classic mint tabbouleh
Prepare the basic recipe, replacing the cilantro with 1 small bunch of chopped fresh mint.

variations

# quinoa with rosemary & bell peppers

see base recipe page 122

### bulgur wheat with rosemary & bell peppers
Prepare the basic recipe, using bulgur wheat in place of the quinoa. Instead of boiling, simply put the bulgur in a bowl, cover with boiling water, and let it stand for 20 minutes before draining.

### quinoa with rosemary, bell peppers & halloumi
Cut 1/2 pound halloumi cheese into 1/3-inch-thick slices, then broil on both sides until golden. Cut into slices, toss into the salad just before serving.

### couscous with rosemary & bell peppers
Prepare the basic recipe, using couscous in place of the quinoa. Instead of boiling, put the couscous in a bowl, mix in 1 tablespoon olive oil and a pinch of salt, then pour in 2 1/3 cups boiling water and let stand for 5 minutes. Fluff up the grains before tossing with the other ingredients.

### quinoa with rosemary, bell peppers & borlotti beans
Prepare the basic recipe, adding 2 (14-ounce) cans borlotti (cranberry) beans, drained, to the salad.

### quinoa with sage & red peppers
Prepare the basic recipe, using 1/2 tablespoon chopped fresh sage in place of the rosemary.

variations

# warm chickpea salad with eggplant & zucchini

see base recipe page 124

**warm flageolet bean salad with eggplant & zucchini**
Prepare the basic recipe, using flageolet beans in place of the chickpeas.

**warm chickpea salad with zucchini & sweet peppers**
Prepare the basic recipe, replacing the eggplant with 2 seeded red or yellow bell peppers cut into large strips.

**warm chickpea salad with eggplant, zucchini & spinach**
Prepare the basic recipe, using 4 handfuls of baby spinach leaves in place of the alfalfa sprouts.

**warm chickpea & tomato salad with eggplant & zucchini**
Prepare the basic recipe, adding 1 1/3 cups cherry tomatoes with the chickpeas and olives.

**warm chickpea & caraway salad with eggplant & zucchini**
Prepare the basic recipe, replacing the fennel seeds with 1 teaspoon caraway seeds.

variations

# rice salad with mozzarella & bell peppers

see base recipe page 126

### rice salad with feta & bell peppers
Prepare the basic recipe, replacing the mozzarella with 1/2 pound roughly crumbled feta cheese.

### rice salad with stilton & bell peppers
Prepare the basic recipe, replacing the mozzarella with 1/2 pound cubed Stilton cheese.

### rice salad with mozzarella, bell peppers & pistachios
Prepare the basic recipe, adding 4 tablespoons roughly chopped pistachio nuts with the broiled peppers and olives.

### rice salad with goat's cheese, bell peppers & pine nuts
Prepare the basic recipe, adding 4 tablespoons toasted pine nuts with the broiled peppers and olives.

variations

# green bean & chickpea salad with cherry tomatoes & red onion

see base recipe page 128

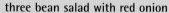

### three bean salad with red onion
Prepare the basic recipe, omitting the chickpeas and tomatoes, and adding 1/2 cup rinsed canned butter beans and 1/2 cup rinsed canned flageolet beans.

### green bean & chickpea salad with lemon dressing
Prepare the basic recipe, adding 1 teaspoon finely grated lemon zest to the dressing.

### chickpea salad with snow peas, cherry tomatoes & red onion
Prepare the basic recipe, using snow peas in place of the green beans. Cook them for 2 minutes only, then refresh in cold water.

### green bean & chickpea salad with thyme dressing
Prepare the basic recipe, replacing the basil with 1 teaspoon fresh thyme leaves.

### borlotti & green bean salad with cherry tomatoes & red onion
Prepare the basic recipe, using drained, rinsed canned borlotti (cranberry) beans in place of the chickpeas.

variations

# lenticchie all'umbra

see base recipe page 130

### lentil & bacon salad with sweet peppers
Prepare the basic recipe, using 8 strips bacon, snipped into small pieces, in place of the pancetta. Replace the tomatoes with 2 seeded and diced red or yellow bell peppers.

### lentil & pancetta salad with fresh herbs
Prepare the basic recipe, adding a small handful of fresh cilantro leaves and 2 tablespoons snipped fresh chives to the skillet with the tomatoes.

### lentil, tomato & pancetta salad with sweet peas
Prepare the basic recipe. Cook 1 cup frozen peas in boiling water for about 3 minutes, then drain, refresh under cold water, and toss into the salad before garnishing with basil.

### spicy lentil & tomato salad
Prepare the basic recipe, adding 1/4 teaspoon crushed dried chile flakes with the garlic and herbs.

variations

# wild rice salad with walnuts & dried cranberries

see base recipe page 132

### wild rice salad with pistachios & dates
Prepare the basic recipe, using 6 tablespoons pistachios and 8 chopped dates in place of the walnuts and cranberries.

### wild rice salad with avocado, walnuts & dried cranberries
Prepare the basic recipe, adding 2 pitted, peeled, and diced avocados with the walnuts and cranberries.

### wild rice salad with watercress, walnuts & dried cranberries
Prepare the basic recipe, adding a large handful of roughly chopped watercress with the walnuts and cranberries.

### wild rice salad with fresh herbs, walnuts & dried cranberries
Prepare the basic recipe, adding a handful of roughly chopped fresh parsley, 1 teaspoon fresh thyme leaves, and 1 tablespoon chopped fresh chives.

### wild rice salad with apple, celery & walnuts
Prepare the basic recipe, using 1 cored, diced apple and 2 sliced celery stalks in place of the cranberries.

variations

# green bean salad with sesame & cilantro

see base recipe page 134

### green bean salad with sesame, cilantro & chile
Prepare the basic recipe, adding 1/2 finely chopped seeded red chile pepper
with the garlic and ginger.

### fava bean salad with sesame & cilantro
Prepare the basic recipe, using shelled fava beans in place of the green
beans. Blanch them for 3–6 minutes until just tender.

### zucchini salad with sesame & cilantro
Prepare the basic recipe, using 3 thickly sliced zucchini in place of the green
beans and blanch for several minutes until just tender.

### green bean & carrot salad with sesame & cilantro
Prepare the basic recipe, replacing half the green beans with 4 carrots, cut
into sticks. Blanch the carrots for 3 minutes, then refresh under cold water.

### green bean salad with cilantro & peanuts
Prepare the basic recipe, using 3 tablespoons roughly chopped peanuts in
place of the sesame seeds.

variations

# bean salad with red onions & parsley

see base recipe page 136

### flageolet bean & red onion salad with balsamic dressing
Prepare the basic recipe, using 2 tablespoons balsamic vinegar in place of the wine vinegar.

### flageolet bean & red onion salad with chives
Prepare the basic recipe, adding 2 tablespoons snipped fresh chives with the parsley.

### butter bean & red onion salad
Prepare the basic recipe, using butter beans in place of the flageolet beans.

### cannellini bean & red onion salad
Prepare the basic recipe, using cannellini beans in place of the flageolet beans.

### flageolet bean, red onion & tuna salad
Prepare the basic salad, stirring 2–2 1/2 cans drained, flaked tuna into the salad with the parsley.

# pasta salads

Popular with kids and adults alike, pasta salads are loved by everyone. Whether you choose plain, flavored, whole wheat, or stuffed pasta to make your salad—it will provide a healthy, sustaining source of energy for you and your family.

# orzo salad with vegetables & feta

see variations page 163

Orzo is a tiny rice-shaped pasta that's particularly popular in Greece. It's great for salads, and this tangy recipe makes an easy lunchbox meal.

| | |
|---|---|
| 1 lb. orzo | 2 yellow bell peppers, diced |
| 1 lb. fresh asparagus | juice and zest of 1/2 lemon |
| 2 tbsp. pine nuts | salt and freshly ground pepper |
| 3 tbsp. olive oil | 2/3 cup feta cheese |
| 12 cherry peppers, halved | fresh basil leaves, to garnish |

Cook the orzo in plenty of boiling, salted water according to the package instructions, until al dente. Drain, refresh in cold water, and drain well. Wash the asparagus and cut at an angle into approximately 1-inch lengths. Toast the pine nuts in a dry skillet until golden brown. Let cool.

Heat the oil in a skillet and sauté the peppers and asparagus for about 2 minutes, stirring. Add the lemon zest and orzo and warm through. Add salt, pepper, and lemon juice to taste.

Spoon onto plates. Scatter with crumbled feta, sprinkle with the toasted pine nuts, and garnish with basil.

*Serves 4*

# tricolor fusilli salad

see variations page 164

Using pasta shapes colored with spinach and tomato can create a stunning salad that's just too appealing to resist.

| | |
|---|---|
| 1 lb. tricolor fusilli | 4 tbsp. olive oil |
| 3/4 lb. green beans | 4 tbsp. white wine vinegar |
| 1 celery stalk, sliced | salt and freshly ground pepper |
| 1 red bell pepper, diced | cayenne pepper |
| generous 1/3 cup pitted and sliced black olives | 8 lettuce leaves, such as butterhead, for serving |

Cook the fusilli in boiling salted water according to the package instructions, until al dente, then drain.

Trim the green beans and blanch in salted water for about 4 minutes, then place immediately in cold water to halt the cooking process. Drain, then cut the beans in half. Blanch the celery for about 2 minutes.

Mix the olive oil, vinegar, salt, pepper, and cayenne pepper together in a large bowl. Add the pasta, beans, celery, red pepper, and olives. Taste and add more salt, pepper, and cayenne if desired. Let marinate for about 15 minutes. Place 2 lettuce leaves on each plate, top with a serving of the salad, and serve.

*Serves 4*

# couscous salad

see variations page 165

Although most people think of it as a grain, light, fluffy couscous is actually a type of pasta. It is fabulous for simple salads because it is able to carry the flavor of other ingredients brilliantly.

about 3 cups vegetable stock
3 cups couscous
1/3 cup raisins
1/3 cup currants
1 red bell pepper, diced
1 green bell pepper, diced
1/3 cup sun-dried tomatoes in oil, roughly
    chopped

1 onion, diced
2 tbsp. white wine vinegar
2 tbsp. lemon juice
3 tbsp. olive oil
salt and freshly ground pepper
1/2 small bunch fresh mint, roughly chopped

Bring the vegetable stock to a boil. Put the couscous, raisins, and currants into a bowl. Pour the boiling stock into the bowl. Let the couscous stand for about 10 minutes, then fluff with a fork.

Put the diced bell peppers, tomatoes, and onion in a serving bowl. Whisk together the vinegar, lemon juice, and olive oil to make a dressing. Season with salt and pepper, and pour it over the vegetables. Add the couscous and mint, toss to combine, and serve.

*Serves 4*

# orecchiette with beans & arugula pesto

see variations page 166

In Italy, the word *orecchiette* means "little ears," which perfectly describes these domed pasta shapes. They require slightly longer cooking than regular pasta and have a deliciously chewy texture.

1 1/2 cup canned kidney
   beans in water
about 1 tbsp. olive oil
1 clove garlic, finely chopped
1/3–1/2 cup white wine
1 2/3 cups vegetable stock
4 1/2 cups (1 lb.) orecchiette

2/3 cup roughly chopped
   fresh spinach
for the pesto:
1 bunch fresh arugula,
   roughly chopped and
   tough stems removed
2 tbsp. pine nuts

1 tbsp. freshly grated
   Parmesan
1 clove garlic
about 6 tbsp. olive oil
sea salt and freshly ground
   pepper

Drain the beans and rinse gently. In a saucepan, heat the olive oil and briefly sauté the garlic. Add the drained beans, then stir in the white wine and stock. Boil vigorously for 10 minutes, then turn down and simmer for 10 minutes. Drain and transfer to a large salad bowl.

Cook the orecchiette according to the package instructions until al dente. Drain and add to the kidney beans.

To make the pesto, put the arugula, pine nuts, Parmesan, garlic, and a little olive oil in a food processor or blender. Process, adding more olive oil in a thin stream, until the pesto is smooth and creamy. Season to taste with salt and pepper.

Add the spinach to the beans and pasta. Then add the pesto and toss to combine. Season to taste before serving.

*Serves 4*

# pasta salad with ham & peas

see variations page 167

Ham and peas are a classic combination—whether in soup, risotto, or as here in this chunky pasta salad. Kids will love it, but so will the grownups.

1 1/3 cups frozen peas
1 large carrot
2 scallions
3/4 lb. caserecce or macaroni
14 oz. kassler (smoked and cured pork loin) or
    turkey ham
3 1/2 oz. cheddar, shredded

pinch of paprika
salt and pepper

for the dressing:
4 tbsp. mayonnaise
scant 1/2 cup sour cream
3/4–1 cup cream

Thaw the peas. Peel the carrot and cut into julienne strips. Trim the scallions and cut at an angle into approximately 1/4-inch rings.

Cook the pasta in plenty of boiling, salted water according to the package instructions, adding the peas, carrots, and scallions after 5 minutes. Continue cooking until the pasta is al dente. Drain in a colander, then refresh in cold water, drain well, and let cool.

Cut the pork (or turkey ham) into approximately 1/2-inch cubes. Add the cheese and ham to the cooled pasta and vegetables, mix, and season well with a pinch of paprika, salt, and pepper.

To make the dressing, mix all the ingredients together. Taste and adjust the seasoning. Pour the dressing over the salad, mix well, and season again. Serve on plates with a garnish of your choice.

*Serves 4*

# farfalle with shrimp & artichokes

see variations page 168

Combining shrimp and artichoke in this simple recipe creates a sophisticated salad that's great for alfresco entertaining or a no-fuss lunch with friends.

3/4 lb. farfalle
3/4 lb. mini-artichokes
juice of 1 lemon
2 ripe tomatoes, quartered, seeds removed
confectioners' sugar
12 raw shrimp, peeled (apart from tail) and
    deveined

1/4 lb. bacon slices, cut in thin strips
1 clove garlic, finely chopped
olive oil
3 tbsp. white wine vinegar
sea salt and freshly ground pepper
freshly grated Parmesan for serving

Cook the farfalle in boiling salted water according to package instructions until al dente. Drain. Clean and quarter the artichokes. Place in cold water with half the lemon juice.

Place the tomatoes on a baking pan lined with parchment paper. Sprinkle with confectioners' sugar. Add the shrimp, drained artichokes, bacon, and garlic to the pan. Drizzle olive oil over everything and sprinkle with salt and pepper. Place under a preheated broiler for about 2 minutes. Turn all ingredients over and broil an additional 2 minutes.

Put the farfalle in a large serving bowl. Add the tomatoes, shrimp, artichokes, bacon, and garlic. Drizzle olive oil over the top and mix in the vinegar and remaining lemon juice. Season with salt and pepper and serve with grated Parmesan.

*Serves 4*

# pasta salad with shrimp

see variations page 169

You can toss this very easy salad together in no time, making it the perfect choice for a midweek supper.

3/4 lb. penne
3 tbsp. ricotta cheese
3 tbsp. white balsamic vinegar
2 tbsp. olive oil

1/2 lb. cooked shrimp
1 bunch fresh cilantro, finely chopped
salt and freshly ground pepper
2 tbsp. freshly grated Parmesan

Cook the penne in boiling salted water according to package instructions until al dente. Drain and cool.

In a serving bowl, mix together the ricotta cheese, balsamic vinegar, and olive oil. Stir until smooth. Add the drained pasta, shrimp, and cilantro, and toss to combine. Season to taste with salt and pepper and sprinkle with the Parmesan before serving.

*Serves 4*

# pasta alla villana

see variations page 170

There are many different types of spiral-shaped pasta such as fusilli, radiatore, and rotini. Any will be delicious in this recipe. This pasta salad can be served warm or cold.

4 1/2 cups (1 lb.) spiral pasta
10 1/2 oz. fresh asparagus
2 tbsp. oil
4 oz. sliced, smoked ham, cut in thin strips
2 chopped garlic cloves
3/4–1 cup vegetable stock

3/4 cup pitted black olives
1/2 cup sun-dried tomatoes in oil, chopped
2 tbsp. chopped fresh marjoram
2 tbsp. chopped fresh thyme
salt and freshly ground pepper
fresh marjoram, to garnish

Cook the pasta in boiling, salted water according to the package instructions. While it is cooking, peel the lower third of each asparagus spear and cut the spears into approximately 1-inch lengths.

Heat the oil in a large saucepan. Sauté the ham, garlic, and asparagus. Add the stock, cover, and cook for about 5 minutes. Then add the olives, tomatoes, herbs, and drained pasta. Toss to combine. Season to taste with salt and pepper.

Serve warm or cold, garnished with marjoram.

*Serves 4*

# greek tortellini salad

see variations page 171

Tortellini are available with a huge variety of fillings—although traditionally they are stuffed with chopped meat or cheese. For this recipe, choose one that will go well with zucchini and sheep cheese, such as spinach and ricotta, sun-dried tomato, or wild mushroom.

2 small–medium zucchini
6 tbsp. olive oil
2 small red bell peppers, diced
1 tsp. finely grated lemon zest
juice of 1 lemon
1 tsp. fresh thyme leaves

1 tsp. chopped fresh rosemary
   leaves
1 tbsp. chopped fresh parsley
salt and freshly ground
   pepper
14 oz. tortellini

1 cup (7 oz.) crumbled feta, to
   garnish
1/2 cup sliced black olives, to
   garnish

Wash the zucchini, quarter lengthwise, and cut into bite-size pieces. Heat 2 tablespoons of the olive oil in a skillet and sauté the diced bell peppers and zucchini for 3–4 minutes. Remove and let cool.

Mix the remaining 4 tablespoons oil with the lemon zest and juice, herbs, salt, and pepper to make a dressing. Mix with the sautéed vegetables and let stand.

Meanwhile, cook the tortellini according to the package instructions. Drain and add to the vegetables. Mix and season to taste. Serve garnished with the feta and olives. Serve warm or room temperature.

*Serves 4*

# orzo salad with vegetables & feta

see base recipe page 147

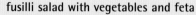

### fusilli salad with vegetables and feta
Prepare the basic recipe, using fusilli in place of the orzo.

### orzo salad with peppers, zucchini & feta
Prepare the basic recipe, using 2 sliced zucchini in place of the asparagus.

### orzo salad with vegetables & goat cheese
Prepare the basic recipe, using diced goat cheese in place of the feta.

### orzo salad with pepper, peas & feta
Prepare the basic recipe, using 1 cup frozen peas in place of the asparagus. Cook peas in boiling water for 2 minutes, then drain and toss with the sautéed peppers and orzo.

### orzo salad with vegetables, feta & mint
Prepare the basic recipe, omitting the basil leaves. Instead, toss 1 1/2 tablespoons chopped fresh mint with the orzo and sautéed vegetables.

variations

# colorful fusilli pasta salad

see base recipe page 148

### tricolor fusilli salad with kidney beans
Prepare the basic recipe, adding 1 (14-ounce) can drained, rinsed kidney beans with the drained pasta and vegetables.

### tricolor fusilli salad with vegetables & capers
Prepare the basic recipe, adding 1 1/2 tablespoons roughly chopped capers to the drained pasta and vegetables.

### tricolor fusilli salad with red-hot chile peppers
Prepare the basic recipe, omitting the cayenne pepper. Instead, add 2 chopped, bottled Peppadew peppers to the drained pasta and vegetables.

### tricolor fusilli salad with fresh herbs
Prepare the basic recipe, adding 3 tablespoons chopped fresh flatleaf parsley, a small handful of torn fresh basil leaves, and 2 tablespoons snipped fresh chives.

variations

# couscous salad

see base recipe page 150

### couscous salad with cranberries & walnuts
Prepare the basic recipe, using 1/2 cup dried cranberries in place of the currants and raisins. Add a handful of walnut pieces to the peppers and tomatoes.

### couscous salad with toasted pine nuts
Prepare the basic recipe, adding 4 tablespoons toasted pine nuts with the peppers and tomatoes.

### couscous salad with goat cheese
Prepare the basic recipe, scattering 1 cup diced goat cheese over the salad.

### couscous salad with fresh apple
Prepare the basic recipe, omitting the currants. Add 2 cored, diced apples to the peppers and tomatoes.

### couscous salad with scallions
Prepare the basic recipe, omitting the onion and adding 5 sliced scallions to the peppers and tomatoes.

variations

# orecchiette with beans & arugula pesto

see base recipe page 152

### orecchiette with beans & fresh basil pesto
Prepare the basic recipe, using 2 small bunches fresh basil in place of
the arugula.

### orecchiette with beans, tomato & spinach
Prepare the basic recipe, adding 1 1/3 cups halved cherry tomatoes with the
spinach.

### orecchiette & bean salad with cheat's pesto dressing
Prepare the basic recipe, omitting the arugula pesto. Instead, stir
2 tablespoons olive oil into 3 tablespoons ready-made pesto, drizzle over the
salad, and toss to combine.

### orecchiette & bean salad with simple mustard dressing
Prepare the basic recipe, omitting the arugula pesto. Instead, whisk
together 2 tablespoons balsamic vinegar with 3 tablespoons olive oil and
1 1/2 teaspoons whole-grain mustard. Drizzle it over the salad and toss.

### orecchiette & bean salad with anchovies
Prepare the basic recipe, adding 8 anchovy fillets, sliced lengthwise, to the
drained beans, pasta, and spinach.

# pasta salad with ham & peas

see base recipe page 154

### pasta salad with smoked trout & peas
Prepare the basic recipe, omitting the ham and cheese. Instead, add 3 flaked
smoked trout fillets.

### pasta salad with ham, peas & blue cheese
Prepare the basic recipe, using 3/4 cup crumbled blue cheese in place of
the cheddar.

### pasta salad with ham, peas & celery
Prepare the basic recipe, adding 3 stalks of celery, sliced, with the peas
and carrot.

### pasta salad with ham, apple & celery
Prepare the basic recipe, omitting the peas. Instead, add 2 stalks sliced celery and
2 cored, diced apples.

### pasta salad with ham, peas & arugula
Prepare the basic recipe. Place a large handful of arugula leaves on each plate
and pile the salad on top.

variations

# farfalle with shrimp & artichokes

see base recipe page 156

### farfalle with crab & artichokes
Prepare the basic recipe, omitting the shrimp. Instead, add 2 cans white crabmeat (drained) to the pasta, broiled artichokes, tomato, and bacon.

### penne with shrimp & artichokes
Prepare the basic recipe, using penne in place of the farfalle.

### spicy farfalle with shrimp & artichokes
Prepare the basic recipe, sprinkling 1/4–1/2 teaspoon crushed dried chile pepper over the tomatoes, artichokes, and shrimp before broiling.

### farfalle with shrimp, artichokes & chives
Prepare the basic recipe, sprinkling 2 tablespoons snipped fresh chives over the salad before tossing.

### farfalle with chicken & artichokes
Prepare the basic recipe, omitting the shrimp. Instead, broil 3 boneless, skinless chicken breasts. Slice them and add to the farfalle, tomatoes, and artichokes before tossing.

# pasta salad with shrimp

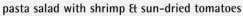

see base recipe page 158

### pasta salad with shrimp & sun-dried tomatoes
Prepare the basic recipe, adding 8 sun-dried tomatoes, drained and snipped into bite-size pieces, with the shrimp.

### pasta salad with shrimp & sugar snap peas
Prepare the basic recipe. While the pasta cooks, blanch 1/2 pound sugar snap peas for about 2 minutes, then drain and refresh under cold water before tossing with the pasta and shrimp.

### pasta salad with lemon–ricotta dressing
Prepare the basic recipe, whisking 1 teaspoon finely grated lemon zest into the dressing.

### pasta salad with ham & ricotta dressing
Prepare the basic recipe, using 1/2 pound diced ham in place of the shrimp.

### pasta salad with shrimp & dill
Prepare the basic recipe, using 3 tablespoons snipped fresh dill in place of the cilantro.

variations

# pasta alla villana

see base recipe page160

### garganelli salad with ham & asparagus
Prepare the basic recipe, using garganelli pasta in place of the spirals.

### pasta salad with smoked salmon & asparagus
Prepare the basic recipe, omitting the ham. Instead, add 4 ounces smoked salmon, cut into strips, with the olives, tomatoes, and herbs.

### pasta salad with spring vegetables & ham
Prepare the basic recipe, using 1/3 pound asparagus, 3/4 cup frozen peas, and 3/4 cup shelled fava beans. Add the peas and beans to the pan with the stock and cook until they are tender.

### pasta salad with asparagus, ham & roasted peppers
Prepare the basic recipe, using a jar (about 9 ounces) roasted red peppers (drained, but not chopped) in place of the sun-dried tomatoes.

### pasta salad with zucchini & ham
Prepare the basic recipe, using 3 sliced zucchini in place of the asparagus and reduce the cooking time to 2 minutes.

variations

# greek tortellini salad

see base recipe page 162

### greek ravioli salad
Prepare the basic recipe, using ravioli in place of the tortellini.

### greek-style penne salad
Prepare the basic recipe, using 3/4 pound penne in place of the tortellini.

### zucchini & tortellini salad
Prepare the basic recipe, omitting the crumbled feta. Instead, serve the salad topped with shavings of Parmesan cheese.

### greek tagliatelle salad
Prepare the basic recipe, using 3/4 pound tagliatelle in place of the tortellini.

# slaws &
# shredded salads

Crisp, crunchy vegetables and fruits such as

cabbage, carrot, and green papaya are perfect for

shredding and turning into tasty slaws and salads.

Whether you go for a classic, creamy coleslaw

or a spicy Asian-style shredded salad, there are

countless delicious recipes to choose from.

# carrot salad with pearl onions & parsley

see variations page 185

This cooked vegetable salad with its light, tangy dressing makes a great accompaniment to broiled meats and fish. It is also a good choice for a light appetizer.

2 tbsp. butter
5 cups (1 3/4 lbs.) carrot sticks
9 oz. pearl onions, peeled
1/3–1/2 cup vegetable stock

4 cloves garlic, sliced
1 bunch fresh parsley, roughly chopped
salt and pepper
white wine vinegar

Heat the butter in a saucepan and sauté the carrot sticks and onions. Add the stock, cover, and cook over medium heat for 5 minutes. Add the sliced garlic to the pan after 2–3 minutes.

When the vegetables are cooked, but still retain a little bite, remove from the heat, mix in the parsley, and season with salt and pepper. Add vinegar to taste and let cool slightly. Put the carrot salad on individual plates and serve warm or cold.

*Serves 4*

# green papaya & chile salad

see variations page 186

This light, zesty salad is a simplified version of the classic spicy papaya eaten in Thailand. It's particularly good served with coconut rice.

1–2 green papayas (about 1 1/2 lbs.)
2 kaffir lime leaves
2 chiles

for the dressing:
zest and juice of 1 lime
2 tbsp. light fish sauce
1 tbsp. brown sugar
2 cloves garlic, sliced

Peel, wash, halve, and seed the papayas. Shred finely, using a mandoline vegetable slicer if available. Finely shred the kaffir lime leaves. Halve and seed the chiles and slice very finely.

To make the dressing, mix the lime zest and juice with the fish sauce and brown sugar. Add the garlic.

Mix the shredded papaya with the dressing and pile into bowls. Sprinkle with the lime leaves and sliced chile and serve.

*Serves 4*

# two-tone coleslaw

see variations page 187

Crisp and crunchy coleslaw is one of those salads that's perfect for every occasion. It's great in winter when other salad vegetables are out of season, but it's a fabulous dish for barbecues and a must for any buffet table or family meal. This coleslaw is especially colorful.

| | | |
|---|---|---|
| 1/2 lb. green cabbage | for the dressing: | pinch sugar |
| 1/2 lb. red cabbage | 2 tbsp. mayonnaise | 2 tbsp. white wine vinegar |
| 1 carrot | 1 tbsp. crème fraîche | 2 tbsp. raisins |
| 1 apple | 1 tsp. dry mustard | salt and pepper |

Wash the green cabbage and the red cabbage and remove the stem. Slice or shred into thin strips. Peel the carrot and the apple. Quarter the apple and remove the core. Grate the apple and the carrot very thinly. Put the cabbage, carrot, and apple in a large serving bowl.

In a small bowl, combine the mayonnaise, crème fraîche, dry mustard, sugar, vinegar, and raisins. Season with salt and pepper. Pour over the salad and toss to combine. Let stand for 15 minutes and season again before serving.

*Serves 4*

# country slaw

see variations page 188

This crunchy and colorful slaw made with crisp raw vegetables has a simple, rustic feel. Make it in late summer when sweet peppers and tender zucchini are at their best.

2 stalks celery, thinly sliced
4 carrots, peeled and cut into matchsticks
2 zucchini, cut into matchsticks
2 red bell peppers, cut into thin strips
1 bunch fresh basil, chopped

for the dressing:
2 tbsp. white balsamic vinegar
2 tbsp. lemon juice
1 tsp. honey
3 tbsp. grapeseed oil or canola oil
salt and freshly ground pepper
fresh basil leaves, to garnish

Put the celery, carrots, zucchini, bell peppers, and chopped basil into a large bowl.

In a small bowl, mix the balsamic vinegar with the lemon juice, honey, and oil. Pour the dressing over the vegetables, and toss to combine. Season to taste with salt and pepper. Serve in individual bowls, garnished with basil.

*Serves 4*

# red cabbage salad with jicama & peppers

see variations page 189

Jicama, native to South America, is a root vegetable with a mild, nutty flavor. It can either be cooked or used raw in salads. This salad goes very well with broiled food.

2 red bell peppers
2 yellow bell peppers
1/2 red cabbage
1 carrot

14 oz. jicama
3 tbsp. olive oil
2 tbsp. white wine vinegar
2 tbsp. fresh lime juice

1 tsp. honey
salt and cayenne pepper
2 tbsp. fresh cilantro leaves

Wash and halve the bell peppers, remove the seeds and the white inner ribs, and cut the flesh into very thin strips. Trim the red cabbage, remove the stalk, and shred the leaves. Peel and shred the carrot and jicama (using a mandoline vegetable slicer if available). Place all the vegetables in a large serving bowl, and toss.

Mix the olive oil, vinegar, lime juice, and honey. Season to taste with salt and cayenne pepper.

Pour the dressing over the salad ingredients, combine, and let stand for at least 1 hour. Garnish with the cilantro before serving.

*Serves 4*

# insalata trevigiana

see variations page 190

This fennel, radicchio, and gorgonzola salad from the Treviso region of Italy is ideal for an elegant appetizer.

2 fennel bulbs
1 head radicchio
1/2 cup roughly chopped walnuts
3/4 cup diced Gorgonzola

for the dressing:
6 tbsp. olive oil
2 tbsp. lemon juice
2 tbsp. white balsamic vinegar
1 tbsp. honey
1/2 bunch fresh parsley, roughly chopped
salt and freshly ground pepper

Cut off the fennel leaves and reserve for the garnish. Wash the bulbs, remove the hard core, and cut the bulbs into thin strips. Put into a serving bowl. Wash and trim the radicchio, shred it (not too finely), and add to the bowl. Add the chopped walnuts and diced Gorgonzola to the bowl.

Make a dressing from the oil, lemon juice, vinegar, honey, and parsley. Season to taste with salt and pepper.

Just before serving, pour the dressing over the salad and mix well. Serve immediately, garnished with the fennel leaves.

*Serves 4*

# asian slaw

see variations page 191

If you like Asian flavors, you'll especially enjoy this light, crisp salad with its sweet-sharp ginger and sesame dressing.

2 carrots
4 cups shredded green cabbage
4 cups shredded red cabbage
1/2 bunch fresh Thai basil

for the dressing:
2 tbsp. sesame seeds
1 tbsp. brown sugar
1 tsp. freshly grated ginger
1 tbsp. sesame oil
1 tsp. sesame paste
juice of 1 lime
1 chile pepper, finely chopped

Peel and shred the carrots, using a mandoline vegetable slicer if available. Put the carrots into a large serving bowl with the shredded cabbage.

To make the dressing, mix the sesame seeds with the brown sugar, grated ginger, sesame oil and paste, lime juice, and finely chopped chile.

Mix the dressing with the shredded cabbage and carrots and let stand for about 15 minutes. Mix in the chopped Thai basil just before serving.

*Serves 4*

# carrot salad with pearl onions & parsley

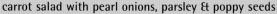
see base recipe page 173

### carrot salad with pearl onions, parsley & poppy seeds
Prepare the basic recipe, sprinkling 1/2 tablespoon poppy seeds over the salad with the vinegar.

### spicy carrot & pearl onion salad
Prepare the basic recipe, adding 1/2 finely chopped, seeded red chile pepper to the pan with the carrots.

### carrot & leek salad
Prepare the basic recipe, using 2 sliced leeks in place of the pearl onions.

### carrot, yellow pepper & pearl onion
Prepare the basic recipe, adding 2 seeded, sliced yellow bell peppers to the pan with the carrots.

variations

# green papaya & chile salad

see base recipe page 174

### carrot, green papaya & chile salad
Prepare the basic recipe, using 1 green papaya and 2 large carrots in place of the original 1–2 papayas.

### spicy carrot & kohlrabi salad
Prepare the basic recipe, using 2 large carrots and 2 kohlrabi (peeled) in place of the papaya.

### spicy green papaya salad with peanuts
Prepare the basic recipe, adding 4 tablespoons roughly chopped peanuts.

### green papaya, chile & chicken salad
Prepare the basic recipe, adding 2 sliced broiled chicken breasts.

### green papaya, chile & shrimp salad
Prepare the basic recipe, adding 1/2 pound cooked, peeled, and deveined shrimp.

variations

# two-tone coleslaw

see base recipe page 176

### blueberry coleslaw
Prepare the basic recipe, using 3 tablespoons dried blueberries in place of the raisins.

### pear coleslaw
Prepare the basic recipe, using 1 firm, ripe pear in place of the apple.

### extra-crunchy coleslaw
Prepare the basic recipe, adding 4 stalks sliced celery to the shredded vegetables before dressing.

### chicken coleslaw
Prepare the basic recipe, adding 3 diced, broiled chicken breasts to the shredded vegetables before dressing.

### pecan coleslaw salad
Prepare the basic recipe, adding a small handful of pecans to the shredded vegetables before dressing.

variations

# country slaw

see base recipe page 178

### country slaw with honey-mustard dressing
Prepare the basic recipe, whisking 1 teaspoon Dijon mustard into
the dressing.

### country slaw with dried cranberries
Prepare the basic recipe, adding 3 tablespoons dried cranberries to the
prepared vegetables.

### country slaw with fresh oranges
Prepare the basic recipe. Cut away the peel from 2 oranges, then slice
between the segments to release the flesh to add to the salad.

### country slaw with apple
Prepare the basic recipe, adding 1 cored, diced apple to the prepared
vegetables.

variations

# red cabbage salad with jicama & peppers

see base recipe page 180

### red cabbage salad with cucumber & peppers
Prepare the basic recipe, using 1 peeled, seeded cucumber in place of the jicama.

### red cabbage salad with nectarines & peppers
Prepare the basic recipe, using 3 pitted nectarines, cut into bite-size pieces, in place of the jicama.

### red cabbage salad with kohlrabi & peppers
Prepare the basic recipe, using 2 peeled kohlrabi in place of the jicama.

### red cabbage salad with daikon & peppers
Prepare the basic recipe, using 1 peeled daikon radish in place of the jicama.

variations

# insalata trevigiana

see base recipe page 182

### fennel, radicchio & orange salad
Prepare the basic recipe, omitting the Gorgonzola. Instead, cut away the peel and white pith from 3 oranges, then cut between the membranes to remove the flesh. Add the pieces to the salad just before dressing.

### fennel, radicchio & goat cheese salad
Prepare the basic recipe, using diced goat cheese in place of the Gorgonzola.

### fennel, radicchio & peach salad
Prepare the basic recipe, omitting the Gorgonzola. Instead, add 3 pitted nectarines, cut into bite-size slices, just before serving.

### fennel, radicchio & gorgonzola salad with black olives
Prepare the basic recipe, adding 1/2 cup black olives with the Gorgonzola.

### fennel, arugula & gorgonzola salad
Prepare the basic recipe, using 2 handfuls of arugula leaves in place of the radicchio.

# asian slaw

see base recipe page 184

### asian-style slaw with chinese leaves
Prepare the basic recipe, replacing the green and red cabbage with 1 shredded head of Chinese cabbage.

### asian slaw with toasted cashews
Prepare the basic recipe, adding a large handful of toasted cashews to the shredded cabbage and carrots.

### asian slaw with fresh cilantro
Prepare the basic recipe, using a large handful of roughly chopped fresh cilantro leaves in place of the Thai basil.

### ruby-red Asian slaw
Prepare the basic recipe, adding 1 finely shredded beet with the shredded cabbage and carrot.

# main course salads

A light, healthy salad containing fresh, leafy
vegetables, sustaining carbohydrates, and essential
protein makes a great choice for a main meal.
Enjoy for lunch or supper, and if you're feeling
extra-hungry, serve with wedges of crusty bread
on the side.

# salade niçoise

see variations page 217

One of the all-time classic salads, niçoise is an easy midweek family supper as well as suitable for entertaining friends.

5–6 oz. fresh green beans
1 clove garlic
1 head radicchio, torn into bite-size pieces
2/3 cup frisée (curly endive), torn into bite-size
   pieces
3 scallions, cut in thin rings
3/4 cup cherry tomatoes, halved

2 hard-boiled eggs, peeled and cut in eighths
1 (6-oz.) can white albacore tuna
1/4 cup pitted and halved black olives
for the dressing:
6 tbsp. olive oil
juice of 1 lemon
salt and freshly ground pepper

Trim the ends of the beans and cook in plenty of boiling, salted water for 5–6 minutes. Drain, refresh in cold water, and drain again.

Rub a large serving bowl with a halved garlic clove. Put the radicchio, frisée, scallions, tomatoes, and eggs into the bowl. Add the drained beans.

Drain and flake the tuna and add to the salad bowl along with the olives. Mix the olive oil and lemon juice to make a dressing and season with salt and pepper. Sprinkle the salad with the dressing and serve.

*Serves 4*

# seafood salad with avocado & bell pepper

see variations page 218

This fresh, zesty seafood salad is wonderful served on a bed of mixed salad leaves and buttered wholemeal bread on the side.

1 1/4 cups (14 oz.) cooked shrimp
7 oz. crabmeat or surimi (imitation crab), cut into pieces
1 cucumber, halved, seeds removed, and diced
2 red bell peppers, diced
2 avocados, diced

for the dressing:
2 limes
1 tsp. brown sugar
3 tbsp. olive oil
sea salt and freshly ground pepper
fresh parsley, to garnish

Put the shrimp, crabmeat or surimi, cucumber, peppers, and avocados into a large serving bowl.

Cut 1 lime into wedges and set aside. Squeeze the other lime into a bowl. Mix the lime juice with the brown sugar and olive oil. Season to taste with sea salt and pepper. Pour the dressing over the salad and toss to combine thoroughly. Let stand for about 10 minutes before serving, garnished with parsley and the lime wedges.

*Serves 4*

# taco salad

see variations page 219

Crispy, crunchy tacos are the perfect accompaniment for this Mexican-inspired spicy salad.

1 3/4 cups ground meat (beef, turkey, or your preference)
1 tbsp. flour
2 tbsp. clarified butter
1 small onion, sliced
1 shallot, sliced
4 ripe tomatoes, diced
1 head crisp lettuce (preferably Batavia, or substitute iceberg), torn

1 carrot, julienned, to garnish
shredded pepper jack cheese, to garnish
homemade or store-bought taco chips, to serve
for the dressing:
good pinch of chili powder
3/4–1 cup sour cream
3 tbsp. white wine vinegar
salt and pepper

Dust the meat with flour, mix loosely, then fry in clarified butter, breaking it up to brown. Add the sliced onion and shallot and fry briefly. Remove pan from heat, and drain the meat.

Mix all the dressing ingredients, season to taste, and put into a bowl. Mix the diced tomatoes with the lettuce and put into individual bowls. Put the meat on top of the lettuce and garnish with the carrot sticks and shredded cheese. Serve with taco chips and the dressing.

*Serves 4*

# rice & pepper salad with broiled chicken breast

see variations page 220

This vibrant yellow salad speckled with red pepper is fragrant and tangy and great for eating at home or for taking to work for lunch at your desk.

2 cups vegetable stock
1/2 tsp. powdered turmeric
1 cup long-grain rice
4 tbsp. corn or canola oil
2 red bell peppers, cut in strips
1 ripe tomato, finely diced
4 tbsp. freshly squeezed lime juice

salt and pepper
1 chile pepper
1 tbsp. freshly chopped cilantro
3–4 boneless, skinless chicken breasts
2 tbsp. sunflower oil (or canola oil)
fresh cilantro or parsley, to garnish

Pour the vegetable stock into a saucepan and add the turmeric. Bring the stock to a boil. Add the rice, stir, cover the pan, and bring the stock back to a boil. Turn the heat down to very low and cook the rice for about 20 minutes, covered (do not lift the lid), until all the liquid is absorbed. Remove the pan from the heat, drain the rice, rinse with cold water, and put into a large salad bowl.

Heat a little corn oil in a skillet and sauté the bell peppers and tomato. Add to the salad bowl.

Season the lime juice with salt and pepper. Whisk the rest of the corn oil into the seasoned lime juice to make a vinaigrette. Wash the chile, slit open lengthwise, remove the seeds and

white inner ribs, and dice finely. Stir into the vinaigrette. Add the dressing to the rice and vegetables and combine. Set aside.

Remove any fat from the chicken breasts, wash, dry, and season with pepper. Heat the sunflower oil in a skillet and fry the chicken on both sides for about 5 minutes, or until cooked through. Remove from the pan. When cool enough to handle, slice the breasts at an angle.

Spoon the rice salad onto individual plates, top with chicken slices, and serve, garnished with cilantro or parsley.

*Serves 4*

# tuna salad with broiled tomatoes & arugula

see variations page 221

Nutty, peppery arugula is a wonderful base for sweet, tender, broiled tomatoes and tuna in this light, flavorsome salad.

1 1/4 lbs. small-to-medium, ripe tomatoes,
   halved crosswise
2 red onions, cut in wedges
small bunch fresh herbs (parsley, lemon balm,
   oregano, rosemary, sage, and thyme), finely
   chopped

1 dried red chile pepper, finely chopped
5 tbsp. olive oil
salt and pepper
4 tbsp. aged balsamic vinegar
2 (6-oz.) cans tuna, drained and flaked
1 large bunch arugula

Put the tomatoes and onions, cut-sides up, on a sheet pan lined with parchment paper or waxed paper. In a bowl, mix the herbs with the chile and half of the olive oil. Season with salt and pepper. Sprinkle the herb–chile mixture over the tomatoes, then broil in the oven (480°F with convection broiler) for 7–10 minutes, watching carefully so they do not burn. Remove and set aside.

Mix the rest of the olive oil with the vinegar and season lightly with salt and pepper. Put a bed of arugula on each plate. Arrange the flaked tuna, tomatoes, and onions on the arugula. Sprinkle the dressing over each salad and serve.

*Serves 4*

# mixed salad with diced tofu & parmesan

see variations page 222

Tofu is a great source of vegetarian protein, making this salad an ideal choice for anyone following a meat-free diet.

1 1/2 cups tofu
3 tbsp. soy sauce
2 tbsp. apple cider vinegar
2 tbsp. soybean oil (or canola)
2 good pinches freshly ground pepper

1 3/4 cups tomatoes, cut into eighths
4 cups mixed lettuce leaves, torn
1 small white onion, diced
1 oz. Parmesan, to garnish

Cut the tofu into 1/2-inch cubes and put into a bowl. Add the soy sauce, vinegar, and 1 tablespoon soybean oil. Sprinkle with pepper and mix well. Marinate the tofu for about 10 minutes, stirring occasionally.

Put the tomatoes and lettuce leaves into a serving bowl and pour the marinade from the tofu over them.

Heat the rest of the soybean oil in a skillet over medium heat. Sauté the diced tofu, turning frequently. Add the onion at the end and sauté briefly. Mix the tofu and onion with the tomatoes and lettuce. Shave the Parmesan over the salad with a vegetable peeler.

*Serves 4*

# spinach salad with lamb

see variations page 223

Tender, juicy lamb is especially sweet and succulent with leafy salads, particularly ones made with dark green spinach leaves.

10 oz. lamb loin fillet
2 tbsp. oil for frying
salt and pepper
10 oz. baby spinach leaves, torn
1/2 head frisée (curly endive), torn
1 red onion, sliced
1/2 bunch fresh chives, to garnish

for the dressing
1/2 shallot, finely chopped
1 clove garlic, finely chopped
4 tbsp. sherry vinegar
1/2 tsp. mustard
1 tsp. honey
6–8 tbsp. olive oil

Heat oil for frying in a skillet and quickly sauté the lamb fillet on both sides over a fairly high heat. Season with salt and pepper, reduce the heat, and fry for an additional 5 minutes. Wrap in aluminum foil and let rest in a very low oven (210°F ) for 5–8 more minutes.

To make the dressing, put the shallot, garlic, vinegar, mustard, honey, and olive oil into a deep bowl and whisk. Toss the spinach, frisée, and onion with the vinaigrette. Thinly slice the lamb fillet. Arrange the lamb slices and salad leaves on plates, alternating the lamb and greens. Garnish with chives before serving.

*Serves 4*

# carpaccio with parmesan & arugula

see variations page 224

Wafer-thin slices of marinated raw beef are an Italian classic known as carpaccio. They're delicious as a salad with peppery arugula leaves and scented porcini oil.

10 1/2 oz. beef tenderloin
juice of 1 lemon, squeezed
salt and freshly ground pepper

6 tbsp. porcini oil (from delicatessen)
Parmesan cheese, to serve
arugula, to serve

Wrap the beef tenderloin in plastic wrap and freeze for about 20 minutes. Slice into wafer-thin slices with a sharp knife. Put each slice between sheets of plastic wrap and pound carefully and evenly with the flat side of a meat mallet. Arrange beef on 4 well-chilled plates.

Mix the lemon juice and salt, then whisk in the oil. Sprinkle the dressing over the carpaccio and season with freshly ground pepper. Scatter with fine Parmesan shavings and arugula leaves.

*Serves 4*

# salmon fillet on potato & sugar snap salad

see variations page 225

This warm salmon salad with new potatoes, sugar snap peas, and cherry tomatoes makes an elegant and colorful meal for two—perfect for no-fuss romancing.

16 oz. small potatoes
1 1/4 cups sugar snap peas
1 cup cherry tomatoes, halved
l clove garlic
1 red chile pepper
1 bunch fresh basil, plus a few leaves
    for garnish

2 tbsp. white wine vinegar
6 tbsp. olive oil, plus more for brushing
salt and freshly ground pepper
2 pieces salmon fillet, each weighing
    about 5–6 oz.

Wash the potatoes well and cook in salted water until tender. Drain, let steam dry, and halve. Top and tail the sugar snap peas and blanch in boiling, salted water for 4 minutes. Drain well. Put the potatoes and peas into a large bowl. Add the tomatoes and toss together.

Peel and roughly chop the garlic. Wash, seed, and finely chop the chile. Wash the basil and shake dry. In a blender or food processor, purée the basil with the garlic, chile, vinegar, and olive oil. Season with salt and pepper. Pour the dressing over the potatoes, peas, and tomatoes, and let stand for a while.

Brush the salmon with a little oil, season with salt and pepper, and cook on a broiler (not too hot) for 2–3 minutes per side.

Arrange the potato salad on individual plates. Top each serving with a salmon fillet and garnish with basil leaves.

*Serves 2*

# chicken salad with spinach & papaya

see variations page 226

Sweet scented papaya and smooth buttery avocado are a wonderful combination in this simple, leafy chicken salad, which makes a fabulous dish for lunch or supper.

2 tbsp. vegetable oil
2 boneless, skinless chicken
　breasts (about 7 oz. each)
1 ripe avocado
1 tbsp. lemon juice
1 ripe papaya

2 1/2 cups fresh spinach, in
　bite-size pieces
1/4 head iceberg lettuce, in
　bite-size pieces
1 red onion, sliced into rings

for the dressing:
2–3 tbsp. butter
2 tbsp. fennel seeds
1 level tsp. sugar
1/4 cup white balsamic
　vinegar
salt and freshly ground
　pepper

Heat the vegetable oil in a skillet, add the chicken breasts, and cook on both sides for about 7 minutes, until cooked through. While the chicken is cooking, make the fennel seed dressing. Melt the butter in a pan, add the fennel seeds, and heat for 1–2 minutes, then sprinkle with sugar and heat until lightly caramelized. Stir in the balsamic vinegar and remove from the stove.

Halve the avocado, remove the pit, cut the fruit into wedges, and remove the skin. Slice the avocado wedges and sprinkle with lemon juice. Peel and halve the papaya and remove the seeds. Cut the fruit into bite-size pieces. Place the spinach, lettuce, onion, avocado, and papaya into a large salad bowl. Slice the chicken (either warm or cold) thinly and toss with the salad ingredients. Sprinkle with the fennel seed dressing.

*Serves 4*

# lobster, grapefuit & avocado salad with beets

see variations page 227

Tangy grapefruit, creamy avocado, and glorious magenta-colored beet offer the perfect partnership with sweet succulent lobster in this luxurious salad.

1/2 cup white wine
1 parsley root, roughly diced
1 stalk celery, roughly diced
1 carrot, roughly diced
1 onion, roughly diced
3 stalks parsley
1 bay leaf
2 sprigs thyme

salt and freshly ground
    pepper
1 lobster (approximately
    1 3/4 lbs.)
for the salad:
1 red beet (approx. 3 1/2 oz.)
3 tbsp. grapeseed oil (or
    canola oil)

juice of 1/2 lemon
1 grapefruit
1 avocado
1/2 cup bite-size mesclun or
    mixed salad leaves (such
    as radicchio, arugula,
    spinach)
sea salt

In a large pot, place 6 cups water and the white wine. Bring to a boil. Add the parsley root, celery, carrot, onion, and herbs. Season with salt and pepper and simmer for about 15 minutes. Plunge the lobster, head first, into the broth and cook for 8–10 minutes, depending on size. Take out and refresh in cold water. Cut the lobster in half lengthwise with a large, sharp knife. Remove the meat from the tail and the claws. Halve the tail.

To make the salad, steam the beet until tender, 25–30 minutes. Cool, peel, and dice. Mix with 1 tablespoon oil and 1 tablespoon lemon juice. Peel the grapefruit with a sharp knife, removing the white pith and skin, and cut out the segments. Peel and halve the avocado, remove the seed, and cut the flesh into wedges.

Arrange the avocado and grapefruit attractively (like the petals of a flower) on 2 plates, alternating avocado and grapefruit segments. Put a handful of salad leaves in the middle and scatter the diced beet around the outside. Put a lobster claw and half of the tail on each plate. Mix the rest of the lemon juice and oil and drizzle it over the salad. Sprinkle with sea salt before serving.

*Serves 2*

# broccoli & cauliflower salad with roquefort dressing

see variations page 228

Blue cheese is a natural partner for broccoli and cauliflower. It's particularly delicious in this creamy, piquant dressing.

1 3/4 cups broccoli florets
1 3/4 cups cauliflower florets
1 cup radishes, quartered
1 1/3 cups frisée (curly endive), in
   bite-size pieces
2 cups halved cherry tomatoes

for the dressing:
1/4 cup Roquefort cheese
5 tbsp. cream
5 tbsp. plain yogurt
2 tbsp. white balsamic vinegar
salt and freshly ground pepper

Cook the broccoli and cauliflower in boiling, salted water for about 3 minutes, refresh in cold water, then drain.

To make the dressing, mash the Roquefort with a fork, then mix with the cream, yogurt, and balsamic vinegar. Season to taste with salt and pepper.

Combine the broccoli, cauliflower, radishes, frisée, and tomatoes. Put salad onto plates. Spoon the dressing over the salad before serving.

*Serves 4*

# chopped ham salad

see variations page 229

This hearty salad containing greens, apple, carrot, ham, nuts, and cheese is a great choice for a simple weekday lunch or supper.

1 apple
2 tbsp. lemon juice
1/2 head radicchio, torn
1/2 head oak-leaf lettuce, torn
1/2 peeled, diced, seeded cucumber
1 grated carrot
1 tbsp. balsamic vinegar

1 tbsp. grapeseed oil (or canola oil)
1 shallot, diced
4 oz. ham, diced
2 tbsp. chopped fresh parsley
2 tbsp. chopped walnuts
1/2 cup grated cheese
salt

Dice the apple and mix it with the lemon juice. Put the apple, radicchio, lettuce, cucumber, and carrot into a salad bowl. Add the vinegar, oil, diced shallot, ham, parsley, walnuts, and cheese. Mix carefully, season to taste with salt, and serve immediately.

*Serves 2*

variations

# salade niçoise

see base recipe page 193

### smoked mackerel niçoise
Prepare the basic recipe, using 2 skinned and flaked smoked mackerel fillets in place of the tuna.

### fresh tuna niçoise
Prepare the basic recipe, omitting the canned tuna. Instead, season 2 fresh tuna steaks, squeeze a little lemon juice over them, and sear in a very hot pan for about 1 minute on each side. Slice the tuna and arrange on top of the salad.

### veggie niçoise
Prepare the basic recipe, omitting the tuna and using 4 hard-boiled eggs instead of 2.

### smoked trout niçoise
Prepare the basic recipe, using 2 flaked smoked trout fillets in place of the tuna.

variations

# seafood salad with avocado & bell pepper

see base recipe page 194

### shrimp salad with avocado & bell pepper
Prepare the basic recipe, using 1 1/4 pounds cooked shrimp in place of the
original shrimp and surimi.

### spicy wasabi salad with avocado & bell pepper
Prepare the basic recipe, whisking 1/4–1/2 teaspoon wasabi paste into the
dressing, according to your taste preference.

### crab salad with avocado & bell pepper
Prepare the basic recipe, using 2 cans white crabmeat in place of the shrimp
and surimi.

### zesty chicken salad with avocado & bell pepper
Prepare the basic recipe, using 4 sliced, broiled chicken breasts in place of
the shrimp and surimi.

variations

# taco salad

see base recipe page 196

### spicy tortilla salad
Prepare the basic recipe, serving the salads with soft flour tortillas in place of the taco chips.

### taco salad with avocado
Prepare the basic recipe, adding 2 peeled, pitted, diced avocados with the tomatoes and lettuce.

### spicy bean taco salad
Prepare the basic recipe, adding 1 (15-ounce) can kidney beans, drained and rinsed, with the tomatoes and lettuce.

### taco salad with sweet peppers
Prepare the basic recipe, adding 2 seeded, diced red peppers with the onion and shallot.

# rice & pepper salad with broiled chicken breast

see base recipe page 198

### rice, pepper & pea salad with broiled chicken
Prepare the basic recipe, adding 1 cup thawed frozen peas to the salad bowl with the peppers.

### rice & pepper salad with ham
Prepare the basic recipe, omitting the chicken. Instead, add 8 ounces diced smoked ham to the salad with the peppers and tomatoes.

### rice & pepper salad with broiled turkey
Prepare the basic recipe, using 3 turkey steaks in place of the chicken.

### rice & pepper salad with tuna
Prepare the basic recipe, omitting the chicken breasts. Instead, top the salad with 2 (6-ounce) cans tuna, drained and flaked.

### rice & green pepper salad with chicken
Prepare the basic recipe, using green peppers in place of red.

# tuna salad with broiled tomatoes & arugula

see base recipe page 200

### broiled tomato & arugula salad with parmesan
Prepare the basic recipe, omitting the tuna and scattering 1 ounce grated or flaked Parmesan over the top of the salad before serving.

### broiled tomato & arugula salad with chicken
Prepare the basic recipe, omitting the tuna. Scatter 3 sliced broiled chicken breasts over the salad before serving.

### broiled tomato & arugula salad with prosciutto
Prepare the basic recipe, omitting the tuna. Instead, snip 8 strips of prosciutto into bite-size pieces and scatter them over the salad before serving.

### broiled tomato & arugula salad with blue cheese & pine nuts
Prepare the basic recipe, omitting the tuna. Instead, scatter 5 1/2 ounces crumbled Stilton or Roquefort and 3 tablespoons toasted pine nuts over the salad before serving.

# mixed salad with diced tofu & parmesan

see base recipe page 202

### mixed salad with tofu & apple
Prepare the basic recipe, adding 1 cored, diced apple with the tomatoes and salad leaves.

### mixed salad with tofu & green beans
Prepare the basic recipe. While the tofu marinates, boil 7 ounces trimmed green beans for about 4 minutes until just tender, then refresh under cold water. Add to the salad with the tomatoes and salad leaves.

### mixed salad with tofu & bean sprouts
Prepare the basic recipe, adding 2 handfuls of bean sprouts with the tomatoes and lettuce leaves.

### mixed salad with ginger-marinated tofu
Prepare the basic recipe, adding 1 teaspoon freshly grated ginger to the marinade.

### mixed salad with spicy chile tofu
Prepare the basic recipe, adding 3/4 seeded, finely chopped red chile pepper to the marinade.

variations

# spinach salad with lamb

see base recipe page 204

### spinach & lamb salad with balsamic dressing
Prepare the basic recipe, using balsamic vinegar in place of sherry vinegar.

### spinach & lamb salad with spiced garlic dressing
Prepare the basic recipe, using 1 teaspoon harissa paste in place of the mustard.

### spinach & lamb salad pitas
Prepare the basic recipe, and serve inside 4 warmed pita breads with extra salad on the side.

### spinach & lamb salad with tomato
Prepare the basic recipe, adding 1 1/3 cups halved cherry tomatoes to the salad leaves.

variations

# carpaccio with parmesan & arugula

see base recipe page 206

### carpaccio with arugula & tomato salad
Prepare the basic recipe, arranging 1 cup halved cherry tomatoes on the plates with the arugula and Parmesan.

### carpaccio with fragrant salad leaves
Prepare the basic recipe, using a mixed herb salad in place of the arugula.

### carpaccio with bitter salad leaves & pear
Prepare the basic recipe, using 3 heads Belgian endive (divided into leaves) in place of the arugula, and arranging 2 sliced pears on the plates with the endive and Parmesan.

### carpaccio with arugula & avocado salad
Prepare the basic recipe, arranging 2 pitted, peeled, sliced avocado on the plates with the arugula and Parmesan.

# salmon fillet on potato & sugar snap salad

see base recipe page 208

### trout, potato & sugar snap salad
Prepare the basic recipe, using trout fillets in place of the salmon fillets.

### smoked mackerel, potato & sugar snap salad
Prepare the basic recipe, omitting the salmon. Instead, top each salad with a peppered smoked mackerel fillet.

### poached egg, potato & sugar snap salad
Prepare the basic recipe, omitting the salmon. Instead, poach 2 eggs in barely simmering water for 4 minutes, then drain well and gently place one on each salad.

### salmon, potato & green bean salad
Prepare the basic recipe, using 1/2 pound trimmed green beans in place of the sugar snap peas.

### salmon, potato, pea & caper salad
Prepare the basic recipe, whisking 1 tablespoon roughly chopped capers into the dressing.

variations

# chicken salad with spinach & papaya

see base recipe page 210

### chicken salad with arugula & mango

Prepare the basic recipe using arugula in place of the spinach, and 1 ripe mango in place of the papaya.

### chicken salad with spinach & kiwi

Prepare the basic recipe using 3 peeled kiwifruits cut into bite-size pieces, in place of the papaya.

### chicken salad with spinach & carrot

Prepare the basic recipe, omitting the papaya. Instead, peel and grate 2 large carrots and toss into the salad with the avocado and onion.

### chicken salad with arugula & tomatoes

Prepare the salad omitting the papaya and using arugula in place of the spinach. Add scant 1 cup halved cherry tomatoes with the avocado and onion.

### chicken salad with spinach, tomatoes & sugar snap peas

Prepare the basic recipe, adding 7 ounces halved cherry tomatoes and large handful sugar snap peas (steamed for 3 minutes, then refreshed under cold water) to the salad with the avocado and onion.

variations

# lobster & avocado salad with beets

see base recipe page 212

### avocado, grapefruit, and beet salad
Prepare the basic recipe, omitting the lobster (and wine, parsley root, celery, carrot, onion, herbs, and seasoning for cooking). Dress and serve as a side salad.

### simple crab and avocado salad
Prepare the basic recipe omitting the lobster (and wine, carrot, onion, herbs, and seasoning for cooking). Instead, top the salad with 1 (7-ounce) can white crab meat.

### avocado, blood orange, beet, and lobster salad
Prepare the basic recipe, using 2 blood oranges in place of the grapefruit.

### avocado and lobster salad with shallot dressing
Prepare the basic recipe, whisking finely chopped 1/4 shallot into the dressing before drizzling over the salad.

# broccoli & cauliflower salad with roquefort dressing

see base recipe page 214

### broccoli and cauliflower salad with fennel dressing
Prepare the basic recipe, omitting the blue cheese dressing. Instead, use the dressing from chicken salad with spinach & papaya (page 211).

### broccoli and cauliflower salad with feta dressing
Prepare the basic recipe, using feta cheese in place of the Roquefort.

### broccoli, cauliflower, and snow peas salad with roquefort dressing
Prepare the basic recipe, adding 7 ounces snow peas to the broccoli and cauliflower for the last minute of cooking time.

### broccoli and cauliflower salad with quail's eggs and roquefort dressing
Prepare the basic recipe, adding 12 peeled, hard-boiled quail's eggs before adding the dressing.

variations

# chopped ham salad

see base recipe page 216

### chopped ham & egg salad
Prepare the basic recipe, spooning the salad onto 2 plates and topping each
serving with a quartered hard-boiled egg.

### crunchy ham salad
Prepare the basic recipe, adding 2 sticks sliced celery and 1 seeded, diced green
bell pepper with the other vegetables. Serve sprinkled with a small handful
of croûtons.

### tropical chopped ham salad
Prepare the basic recipe, adding 3 diced slices canned pineapple in place of
the apple.

### fragrant chopped ham salad
Prepare the basic recipe, adding a handful of chopped fresh cilantro with
the parsley.

# asian style salads

Crisp, refreshing, spicy salads are popular throughout Asia. They're delicious served as an accompaniment to Asian-style curries and stir-fries, or as a main meal with rice or noodles. For an Asian-themed meal, they can make a great choice for an appetizer.

# beef salad with thai basil

see variations page 247

Thinly sliced marinated beef makes a great addition to this spicy and fragrant tomato and herb salad. For a main meal, serve it with rice or noodles.

2 tbsp. sunflower oil
14 oz. beef sirloin
1 tbsp. honey
2 tbsp. soy sauce
1 bunch fresh Thai basil
1 bunch fresh mint
1 tbsp. rice vinegar

1 tbsp. sesame oil
2 chile peppers, finely shredded
4 ripe tomatoes, seeded and sliced
2 scallions, chopped
2 cloves garlic, finely chopped
2 tbsp. light soy sauce, or to taste

Heat the oil in a skillet and quickly sauté the meat on all sides over a fairly high heat. Remove the meat from the skillet. Mix the honey with the soy sauce and brush the meat with the mixture. Now put into a preheated oven (325°F) for 20–30 minutes, until medium-rare, or as desired. Take out of the oven and let cool. Then slice thinly.

Wash the basil and mint and shake dry. Pick the leaves from the stalks. Slice or chop the leaves, if desired.

Mix the rice vinegar with the sesame oil, basil and mint leaves, chile peppers, tomatoes, scallions, and garlic. Add light soy sauce to taste and mix with the sliced meat. Serve the salad in bowls.

*Serves 4*

# beef with cabbage & zucchini salad

see variations page 248

This simple warm salad is great served as part of a selection of Asian-style dishes such as stir-fries or noodle dishes.

1 head of Chinese cabbage
oil for frying
1 zucchini, sliced
salt and freshly ground pepper
1 lb. beef tenderloin, cut into thin strips

2 shallots, cut into rings
1 clove garlic, finely chopped
scant 1/4 cup sherry
3 tbsp. balsamic vinegar
fresh mint and cilantro leaves, to garnish

Wash the Chinese cabbage, remove the stalk, and finely shred the leaves. Cover each plate with a bed of cabbage leaves.

Heat a little oil in a skillet and fry the zucchini on both sides for about 2 minutes. Season with salt and pepper.

Heat a little oil in another skillet and sauté the beef strips on both sides for about 1 minute. Take them out of the pan and arrange on the cabbage with the zucchini. Sauté the garlic and shallots in the fat left from frying the beef, and add them to the meat. Deglaze the skillet with sherry and balsamic vinegar, season with salt and pepper, and drizzle over the salad. Serve garnished with mint and cilantro leaves.

*Serves 4*

# thai salad with squid, pork & chile dressing

see variations page 249

Fragrant and spicy, this salad is terrific for lunch or supper. It's particularly good served with steamed rice or coconut rice.

14 oz. pork fillet
14 oz. squid
1 tbsp. corn oil
2 cloves garlic, sliced
2 finely chopped chile peppers
4 tbsp. rice wine
3/4–1 cup chicken stock
1 tsp. honey

1 tsp. finely grated fresh gingerroot
2 tbsp. light soy sauce, plus more to taste
2 shallots, thinly sliced
2 tbsp. rice vinegar
1 tbsp. sesame oil
1 tbsp. chopped fresh mint, to garnish
1 tbsp. chopped fresh cilantro, to garnish

Cut the pork into thin strips and cut squid into scored bite-size pieces.

Heat the corn oil in a large skillet. Sauté the garlic for a few minutes. Add the chopped chile peppers and cook briefly. Pour in the rice wine and chicken stock and deglaze the skillet. Add the honey, ginger, and 2 tablespoons soy sauce. Stir, then add the strips of pork and squid. Cover and cook gently over a very low heat for just a few minutes; watch that the squid does not get rubbery. Put the mixture into a serving bowl.

Mix together the shallots, rice vinegar, and sesame oil, then pour this dressing into the serving bowl. Toss to combine. Let the salad cool. Before serving, season again with soy sauce and garnish with a sprinkling of mint and cilantro.

*Serves 4*

# sweet & sour cucumber & onion salad with chile

see variations page 250

Honey, chile, and cider vinegar make an irresistibly tangy dressing for this light and refreshing salad. Serve as an accompaniment to an Asian-style meal or with grilled fish or chicken on a hot summer night.

1 cucumber
1 red onion, sliced lengthwise
4 tbsp. apple cider vinegar
2 tbsp. canola oil

1 tbsp. honey
1 dried chile pepper, crushed
salt

Peel the cucumber, halve lengthwise, scrape out the seeds, and slice.

Put into a bowl with the sliced onion, cider vinegar, oil, and honey. Toss to mix. Add the crushed chile pepper, season to taste with salt, and serve.

*Serves 2*

# egg noodle salad with sesame chicken & snow peas

see variations page 251

This main meal salad is delicious warm or cold. Try taking it to work for lunch or to a picnic.

2 1/2 cups carrot sticks
2 1/2 cups halved snow peas
7 oz. Chinese egg noodles
salt and freshly ground pepper
4 boneless, skinless chicken breasts
    (approx. 1 lb. 4 oz.)
4 tbsp. oil

2–3 tbsp. sesame seeds
2 tsp. freshly grated gingerroot
1/2 cup vegetable stock
1/3 cup soy sauce
2 tbsp. white wine vinegar
1 tsp. sambal oelek chile paste
pinch of sugar

Blanch the carrots and snow peas in boiling, salted water for about 3 minutes, then drain, refresh in cold water, and drain well. Cook the noodles according to the package instructions, then drain, refresh in cold water, and drain well.

Season the chicken breasts with salt and pepper. Heat 2 tablespoons oil in a large skillet and fry the chicken breasts for about 5 minutes on each side. Sprinkle with sesame seeds and toss a few times to coat on all sides. When cooked, remove from the pan.

Mix the ginger with the stock, soy sauce, the remaining 2 tablespoons oil, vinegar, sambal oelek, and sugar. Mix the dressing with the noodles and vegetables in a large bowl. Slice the chicken. Serve the salad in individual bowls with the sliced chicken on top.

*Serves 4*

# asian noodle salad

see variations page 252

Garlic, ginger, scallions, and fresh Thai basil come together in this simple salad to create an aromatic, fragrant Asian-style flavor.

| | |
|---|---|
| 4 1/2 cups (14 oz.) Chinese egg noodles | 2 cups shredded bok choy |
| 1 1/3 cups fresh green beans | 3/4–1 cup chicken stock |
| oil for frying | 2 1/2 cups sliced shiitake mushrooms |
| 2 cloves garlic, finely chopped | 1 bunch fresh Thai basil, roughly chopped |
| 1 tsp. freshly grated ginger | light soy sauce |
| 1 bunch scallions, chopped into rings | ground chili pepper |

Cook the noodles according to the package instructions until al dente. Drain, refresh in cold water, and drain again. Wash and trim the beans and blanch in boiling, salted water for 3–4 minutes. Drain, refresh in cold water, and cut into pieces.

Heat a little oil and sauté the beans, garlic, and ginger. Add the scallions and bok choy and sauté briefly. Add the stock and cook for about 20 minutes. The liquid should almost completely evaporate. Add the mushrooms about 5 minutes before the end of the cooking time. Stir in the noodles and basil, add soy sauce and chili pepper to taste, and serve.

*Serves 4*

# vermicelli salad

see variations page 253

Fine vermicelli noodles make a fabulous base for salads. They are wonderful here, dressed in a ginger and sesame dressing scented with fresh herbs.

scant 1 lb. package vermicelli
1 1/2 cups snow peas
1 tbsp. sesame oil
1 tsp. freshly grated ginger
2 tbsp. rice vinegar

3/4 cup sliced radishes
7 oz. baby corn
light soy sauce
1 bunch fresh Thai basil, roughly chopped
2 tbsp. snipped chives

Cook the vermicelli according to the package instructions. Drain, refresh in cold water, and drain again.

Wash and trim the snow peas and blanch in boiling, salted water for about 1–2 minutes. Drain, refresh in cold water, and drain again.

Mix the sesame oil with the ginger and vinegar. Add the snow peas, radishes, baby corn, and vermicelli. Toss to combine. Add soy sauce to taste. Let stand for about 10 minutes, then sprinkle with the Thai basil and chives and serve.

*Serves 4*

# chicken & shrimp salad with vegetables & noodles

see variations page 254

This lightly spiced, fragrant salad packed with chicken, shrimp, noodles, and tender vegetables makes a great choice as a main dish salad.

| | |
|---|---|
| 1 boneless, skinless chicken breast | 1/2 cup bean sprouts |
| 1 carrot | 1 tbsp. freshly grated gingerroot |
| 1 red bell pepper | 1/4 lb. peeled and deveined shrimp |
| 1/4 lb. snow peas | 2–4 oz. Chinese egg noodles, cooked |
| 2 scallions | 1 tbsp. sesame seeds, lightly toasted |
| 1 clove garlic | light soy sauce |
| 1 tbsp. sesame oil | chile sauce |

Cut the chicken breast into bite-size pieces. Peel carrot and cut lengthwise into thin slices, then cut the slices into tiny sticks. Cut red pepper into thin strips. Blanch the snow peas for about 2 minutes in boiling salted water, then place immediately in cold water to stop the cooking process. Drain well. Chop the scallions into small pieces. Finely chop the garlic. Set aside until ready to cook.

Heat the oil in a large skillet. Add the chicken breast pieces and stir-fry. After about 2 minutes, add the carrot sticks and red pepper, stir-fry for another couple of minutes, and finally add the snow peas, scallions, garlic, bean sprouts, ginger, and shrimp.

Stir-fry everything for about 6 minutes until cooked but still a little crisp. Add the Chinese egg noodles, toss around a little, and then mix in the lightly toasted sesame seeds. Season with soy sauce and chile sauce and serve.

*Serves 2*

# tuna sashimi salad

see variations page 255

Delicate slices of raw tuna are delicious served on top of this Japanese-inspired salad, which is redolent of Asian flavors.

4 1/2 oz. cellophane noodles
2 tbsp. butter
1/2 small onion, thinly sliced lengthwise
6 tbsp. dark soy sauce
1 tbsp. oyster sauce
1/2-inch-piece fresh ginger, finely grated

1–2 tsp. rice vinegar
pinch of sugar
10 1/2 oz. very fresh tuna fillet
1 bunch arugula, washed
2 tsp. black sesame seeds, to garnish
1/2 lime, sliced, to garnish

Soak the cellophane noodles in plenty of lukewarm water according to package directions. Drain the noodles and cut into smaller pieces with scissors if desired.

Heat 1 tablespoon butter in a skillet and sauté the onion until translucent. Remove the onion and set aside. Heat the rest of the butter in the skillet, add the soy sauce and oyster sauce, and boil to reduce slightly. Stir in the ginger and rice vinegar, and add sugar to taste.

Cut the tuna into 6 neat slices.

Put the cellophane noodles and onions on 2 plates and sprinkle with the soy sauce and ginger dressing. Top with the arugula and arrange 3 slices of tuna on top of each serving. Sprinkle with sesame seeds and garnish with lime slices before serving.

*Serves 2*

variations

# beef salad with thai basil

see base recipe page 231

### beef salad with tomatoes, cucumber & thai basil
Prepare the basic recipe, adding 1/2 cucumber, sliced lengthwise, seeded, and sliced, with the tomatoes.

### beef salad with tomatoes, bean sprouts & thai basil
Prepare the basic recipe, adding 3 handfuls of mung bean sprouts with the tomatoes.

### beef salad with tomatoes, carrots & thai basil
Prepare the basic recipe, adding 2 grated carrots with the tomatoes.

### beef salad with thai basil & peanuts
Prepare the basic recipe, sprinkling 3 tablespoons roughly chopped peanuts over the finished salad.

variations

# beef with cabbage & zucchini salad

see base recipe page 232

### ginger beef, cabbage & zucchini salad
Prepare the basic recipe, sautéing 1 teaspoon grated fresh ginger with the garlic and shallot.

### beef, cabbage & zucchini salad with wasabi
Prepare the basic recipe, stirring 1/4 teaspoon wasabi paste into the sherry and balsamic vinegar mixture.

### beef, cabbage & zucchini salad with scallions
Prepare the basic recipe, sprinkling the finished salad with 3 finely sliced scallions.

### spicy beef, cabbage & zucchini salad
Prepare the basic recipe, adding 1 sliced, seeded red chile pepper to the garlic and shallots 1 minute before the end of cooking time.

variations

# thai salad with squid, pork & chile dressing

see base recipe page 234

### thai salad with squid, pork, bean sprouts & chile dressing
Prepare the basic recipe, tossing 2 large handfuls of mung bean sprouts into the salad just before serving.

### thai salad with pork, prawn & chile dressing
Prepare the basic recipe, omitting the squid. Add 14 ounces raw, peeled, and deveined tiger prawns (or jumbo shrimp) to the pork about 2 minutes before the end of cooking time. Toss over the heat until the prawns are pink and the pork is cooked through.

### sesame thai salad with squid, pork & chile dressing
Prepare the basic recipe. To serve, toast 2 tablespoons sesame seeds in a dry frying pan for a minute or two until golden, then sprinkle them over the salad.

### cashew thai salad with squid, pork & chile dressing
Prepare the basic recipe, scattering a handful of toasted cashews over the salad just before serving.

### thai salad with squid, pork, chinese cabbage & chile dressing
Prepare the basic recipe. To serve, shred a Chinese cabbage and divide among 4 plates, then spoon the salad on top.

variations

# sweet & sour cucumber & onion salad with chile

see base recipe page 236

### sweet & sour cucumber & onion salad with chile & cilantro
Prepare the basic recipe, adding a small handful of fresh cilantro with the chile.

### sweet & sour cucumber & onion salad with chile & basil
Prepare the basic recipe, adding a small handful of torn fresh basil leaves with the chile.

### sweet & sour cucumber & onion salad with chives
Prepare the basic recipe, adding 1 tablespoon snipped fresh chives in place of the chile.

### sweet & sour cucumber, tomato & onion salad with chile
Prepare the basic recipe, adding 2 ripe tomatoes cut into bite-size pieces with the cucumber.

### sweet & sour cucumber, pear & onion salad with chile
Prepare the basic recipe, adding 2 thinly sliced peeled, cored pears with the cucumber.

variations

# egg noodle salad with sesame chicken & snow peas

see base recipe page 238

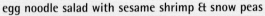

### egg noodle salad with sesame shrimp & snow peas
Prepare the basic recipe, using 10 ounces raw, shelled, deveined large shrimp instead of the chicken. Fry them for 2–3 minutes until pink and cooked through before sprinkling them with the sesame seeds.

### egg noodle salad with sesame chicken & broccoli
Prepare the basic recipe, using 1/2 pound fresh broccoli florets in place of the snow peas.

### egg noodle salad with sesame chicken & cauliflower
Prepare the basic recipe, using 1/2 pound fresh cauliflower florets in place of the snow peas.

### egg noodle salad with sesame chicken, snow peas, & scallions
Prepare the basic recipe, sprinkling the salad with 5 sliced scallions before dressing.

### egg noodle salad with sesame chicken & green peppers
Prepare the basic recipe, omitting the snow peas. Instead, add 2 sliced, seeded green peppers to the noodles and carrots before dressing.

variations

# asian noodle salad

see base recipe page 240

### asian rice noodle salad
Prepare the basic recipe, using 10 ounces rice noodles in place of the egg noodles.

### asian noodle salad with fresh cilantro
Prepare the basic recipe, using fresh cilantro in place of the Thai basil.

### asian noodle salad with cashews
Prepare the basic recipe, adding 2 handfuls of cashews to the pan with the garlic and ginger.

### asian noodle salad with shrimp
Prepare the basic recipe, adding 10 ounces cooked, peeled shrimp with the cooked noodles.

### asian noodle salad with chicken
Prepare the basic recipe, adding 2 sliced, broiled chicken breasts with the cooked noodles.

# vermicelli salad

see base recipe page 243

### egg noodle salad with snow peas, baby corn & radishes
Prepare the basic recipe, using egg noodles in place of the rice noodles.

### spicy vermicelli salad with fresh chile
Prepare the basic recipe, adding 1/2 seeded, finely chopped red chile pepper to the dressing.

### vermicelli salad with peanuts
Prepare the basic recipe, sprinkling 2 tablespoons chopped peanuts over the top of the finished salad.

### vermicelli salad with sweet peppers, baby corn & radishes
Prepare the basic recipe, using 2 seeded red peppers cut into strips in place of the snow peas. (Do not blanch them; simply use raw.)

### vermicelli salad with carrots, baby corn & radishes
Prepare the basic recipe, using 3 carrots sliced into sticks in place of the snow peas.

variations

# chicken & shrimp salad with vegetables & noodles

see base recipe page 244

### seafood salad with vegetables & noodles
Prepare the basic recipe, omitting the chicken. Use 1/2 pound cooked, prepared seafood (such as shrimp, mussels, and squid) in place of the shrimp.

### chicken salad with vegetables & noodles
Prepare the basic recipe, using 2 chicken breasts and omitting the shrimp.

### duck salad with vegetables & noodles
Prepare the basic recipe, using 2 duck breasts in place of the chicken and omitting the shrimp.

### vegetable noodles with cashews
Prepare the basic recipe, omitting the chicken and shrimp. Instead, add 2 handfuls of cashews to the pan with the vegetables.

variations

# tuna sashimi salad

see base recipe page 246

### tiger prawn noodle salad
Prepare the basic recipe, using 5 1/2 ounces cooked, shelled tiger prawns or jumbo shrimp in place of the tuna.

### asian-style crab salad
Prepare the basic recipe, replacing the tuna with canned white crabmeat.

### asian-style tofu salad
Prepare the basic recipe, topping the salad with 5 1/2 ounces marinated deep-fried tofu pieces in place of the tuna.

### tuna sashimi salad with pickled ginger
Prepare the basic recipe, sprinkling the finished salad with 1 tablespoon pickled ginger.

### tuna sashimi salad with wasabi dressing
Prepare the basic recipe, adding 1/4 teaspoon wasabi paste to the dressing.

# fruit salads

Packed with vitamins, fiber, and health-giving nutrients, fruit salads can be crisp and juicy or sweet and succulent, but what they all have in common is their incredible versatility. Enjoy them for breakfast, as a healthy dessert, or a guilt-free snack.

# cubed melon

see variations page 273

This mixed melon salad—delightful on a hot summer day—also makes a stunning, healthy dessert for a special dinner party.

4 different ripe melons (such as watermelon,
    honeydew, cantaloupe, Galia)
white balsamic vinegar (optional)

Peel and seed wedges of each melon and cut the flesh into approximately 1-inch cubes (27 in all). There will be about 1 1/2 cups of each melon.

Assemble the cubes into one large cube, mixing up the different types. If you wish, serve sprinkled with a little white balsamic vinegar.

*Serves 4*

# exotic fruit salad

see variations page 274

This fresh fruit salad made with exotic tropical fruits and a zingy lime dressing is the perfect dessert any time.

1 dragon fruit (pitahaya)
1 avocado
12 lychees
1 star fruit (carambola)

2 kiwifruit
1 Asian pear
1 tbsp. brown sugar
juice of 1 lime

Within half an hour before serving, prepare the fruit for the salad. Halve the dragon fruit and cut out balls with a melon baller. Peel and halve the avocado, remove the seed, and slice the fruit. Peel the lychees and remove the seed. Wash and slice the star fruit. Peel and slice the kiwis. Wash, halve, and core the Asian pear, and cut into wedges. Put all the fruit into a serving bowl.

Mix the brown sugar with the lime juice, then mix with the fruit. Let stand for about 15 minutes, then serve.

*Serves 4*

# colorful fruit salad with black pepper

see variations page 275

Olive oil and black pepper may sound like odd additions for a fruit salad, but it tastes delicious and really brings out the flavors of the sweet, juicy fruit.

2 dragon fruit (pitahaya)
2 kiwifruit
8 lychees
1 ripe mango
1/2 ripe honeydew melon

4 tbsp. extra-virgin olive oil
juice of 2–3 limes
freshly ground black pepper
a few cape gooseberries (physalis), to decorate

Cut into the dragon fruit at the top and remove the skin. Halve the fruit lengthwise, then cut into large wedges. Peel the kiwis and cut in half. Peel the lychees, halve them, and remove the seed. Peel the mango, remove the seed, and cut into slices. Peel the honeydew melon, remove the seeds, and cut into thin slices.

Arrange the fruit decoratively on glass plates or dessert plates. Drizzle olive oil and lime juice over the top. Season with freshly ground pepper, decorate with the cape gooseberries, and serve immediately.

*Serves 4*

# mediterranean fruit salad with spices & pistachios

see variations page 276

This simple salad of sweet Mediterranean fruits, sharp grapefruit, and warm spices is lovely as a dessert or for a weekend breakfast.

1/4 lb. black grapes
2 figs
1 pear
4 dried dates
2 red grapefruit

1 pinch ground cardamom
1 pinch ground cinnamon
juice of 1 lime
1 tbsp. chopped pistachios, to decorate

Wash and halve the grapes lengthwise and remove the seeds. Cut the figs into bite-size pieces. Wash the pear, remove the core, and cut into slices. Remove the pits from the dates and cut into small pieces. Cut the grapefruit into segments.

Place the cut fruit into a serving bowl. Mix the spices with the freshly squeezed lime juice, then pour the mixture over the fruit. Toss well to combine. Sprinkle with chopped pistachios and serve immediately.

*Serves 2*

# blueberry & papaya salad with toasted almonds

see variations page 277

Try this light, refreshing fruit salad for breakfast with Greek yogurt and a glass of freshly squeezed fruit juice.

1/2 lb. fresh blueberries
2 ripe papayas
1/4 lb. blanched almonds
2 tbsp. chopped fresh basil leaves

2 tbsp. agave syrup (from a health food store)
    or honey
1 tbsp. freshly squeezed lemon juice

Wash and sort the blueberries. Peel and halve the papayas, remove the seeds, and dice the flesh. Toast the almonds in a dry frying pan until golden brown, then let cool.

Mix the blueberries and diced papaya with the basil, agave syrup, and lemon juice. Chill for about 30 minutes. Stir in the toasted almonds shortly before serving.

*Serves 4*

# fruit salad with coconut milk

see variations page 278

The addition of coconut milk gives this fresh, fruity salad a deliciously sweet and creamy flavor. It also makes a great dessert for anyone on a dairy-free diet.

2 blood oranges
1 baby pineapple
1 apple
2 kiwifruit
1 banana

2/3 cup unsweetened coconut milk
1 tbsp. honey
freshly squeezed lemon juice
seeds from 1 pomegranate
1 tbsp. chopped fresh cilantro

Peel, halve, and slice the blood oranges. Peel, trim, and dice the pineapple. Peel, quarter, core, and dice the apple. Peel and dice the kiwifruits. Peel and slice the banana.

In a large serving bowl, mix all the fruit with the coconut milk, honey, and lemon juice. Taste and add more honey or lemon if desired. Mix in the pomegranate seeds and cilantro and serve.

*Serves 4*

# fig & nectarine salad

see variations page 279

Tender figs and juicy nectarines make a fabulous combination in this cinnamony, rum-spiked salad. Serve it for a dinner party or a special dessert.

| | |
|---|---|
| 8 figs | juice of 1 lime |
| 3 nectarines | pinch of cinnamon |
| 1 tbsp. honey | 1 1/3 fl. oz. (1 scant jigger) rum |

Wash and dry the figs and cut them into slices. Wash the nectarines and cut them in half. Remove the seed and cut into thin wedges. Put the figs and nectarines into a serving bowl.

Mix the lime juice, cinnamon, and rum together. Pour the mixture over the fruit, mix thoroughly, and let marinate for about 10 minutes before serving.

*Serves 4*

# poached fruit compôte

see variations page 280

A cooked fruit compôte makes a wonderful alternative to a fresh fruit salad. It is good served as dessert or at a brunch buffet.

1/2 cup sugar
juice and grated zest of 1 orange
1/3–1/2 cup port
3/4–1 cup red wine
2 whole cloves
1 cinnamon stick

4 small pears, peeled and halved
4 small peaches, quartered
4 cups rhubarb in 1 1/2-inch slices
honey, to taste
crushed nut brittle, to decorate

Put the sugar into a saucepan and heat until it caramelizes. Stir in the orange juice, port, and red wine. Add the cloves, cinnamon stick, orange zest, and halved pears. Poach for about 10–15 minutes, then add the peaches and rhubarb. Cover and poach for an additional 5 minutes.

With a slotted spoon, remove the fruit from the liquid and set aside. Gently simmer the liquid, stirring occasionally, until it has the consistency of a syrup. Remove the cinnamon stick, cloves, and orange zest, and let it cool slightly.

Arrange the fruit on plates and add a little of the warm syrup. Drizzle with a little honey, sprinkle with nut brittle, and serve.

*Serves 4*

# creamy rice pudding fruit salad

see variations page 281

Sweet and creamy rice pudding makes a rich and luscious base for this fresh and fruity salad.

about 1 1/2 cups milk
1 tsp. pure vanilla extract
1/3 cup sugar
pinch of salt
piece of lemon peel

3/4 cup uncooked rice
2 kiwifruit, peeled and sliced
1 1/4 cups fresh raspberries
2 ripe peaches, diced
2 tbsp. honey
fresh mint leaves, to decorate

Put the milk into a saucepan with the vanilla extract, sugar, salt, and lemon peel. Bring to a boil. Sprinkle in the rice, cover, and cook over a low heat for 20–25 minutes, stirring as little as possible. Remove from the heat when all the liquid is absorbed, but the grains of rice are still separate. Let cool without a lid.

Prepare the fruit just before serving. Gently mix the cold rice with the fruit and honey. Serve decorated with mint.

*Serves 4*

# cubed melon

see base recipe page 256

### cubed melon with ginger
Prepare the basic recipe, sprinkling the melon cubes with 1/2 teaspoon ground ginger before assembling into a large cube.

### cubed melon with mint
Prepare the basic recipe, decorating the melon cube with fresh mint sprigs.

### cubed melon with raspberries
Prepare the basic recipe, surrounding the melon cube with 2 cups fresh raspberries.

### cubed melon with blueberries
Prepre the basic recipe, surrounding the melon cube with 2 cups fresh blueberries.

### cubed melon with lime
Prepare the basic recipe, tossing the melon cubes in the juice of 1 lime before assembling into a large cube.

variations

# exotic fruit salad

see base recipe page 258

### pineapple, lychee & dragon fruit salad
Prepare the basic recipe, omitting the avocado, star fruit, kiwi, and Asian pear, and instead using 1 fresh pineapple (peeled, cored, and eyes removed), cut into bite-size pieces.

### mango, lychee, starfruit & kiwi salad
Prepare the basic recipe, omitting the dragon fruit, avocado, and Asian pear, and instead using 2 ripe mangoes (peeled and pitted), cut into bite-size pieces.

### exotic fruit salad with fresh mint
Prepare the basic recipe, sprinkling the fruit with 1 tablespoon chopped fresh mint before dressing.

### exotic fruit salad with stem ginger dressing
Prepare the basic recipe, adding 2 chopped pieces stem ginger in syrup to the lime juice mixture.

### exotic fruit salad with banana
Prepare the basic recipe, replacing the avocado with 2 peeled, sliced bananas.

# colorful fruit salad with black pepper

see base recipe page 260

### colorful fruit salad with chile
Prepare the basic recipe, replacing the black pepper with a pinch of crushed dried chile flakes.

### colorful fruit salad with cinnamon
Prepare the basic recipe, omitting the olive oil and black pepper. Instead, sprinkle the fruit with 1/4 teaspoon ground cinnamon before drizzling with the lime juice; toss to combine.

### colorful fruit salad with fresh basil
Prepare the basic recipe, adding a small handful of torn fresh basil leaves to the salad with the lime juice and olive oil.

### colorful fruit salad with borage flowers
Prepare the basic recipe, decorating the finished salad with 12 borage flowers.

### colorful fruit salad with cucumber
Prepare the basic recipe, omitting the dragon fruit and instead using 1 peeled, seeded cucumber cut into bite-size chunks.

# mediterranean fruit salad with spices and pistachio nuts

see base recipe page 262

### spiced orange & date salad
Prepare the basic recipe, omitting the grapes, figs, pear, and grapefruit. Instead, cut away the peel and pith from 4 oranges, then slice and arrange on a serving plate. Sprinkle with the dates, dressing, and nuts.

### spiced grape, fig & pear salad
Prepare the basic recipe, replacing the grapefruit with 2 extra figs and 1 extra pear.

### spiced grape, peach & fig salad
Prepare the basic recipe, omitting the pear, dates, and grapefruit. Instead, add 1 extra fig and 2 peeled, pitted peaches cut into bite-size wedges.

### mediterranean fruit salad with spices & walnuts
Prepare the basic recipe, using 2 tablespoons roughly chopped walnuts in place of the pistachio nuts.

# blueberry & papaya salad with toasted almonds

see base recipe page 264

### raspberry & papaya salad with toasted almonds
Prepare the basic recipe, using raspberries in place of the blueberries.

### strawberry & papaya salad with toasted almonds
Prepare the basic recipe, using strawberries (halved or quartered if large) in place of the blueberries.

### blueberry & mango salad with toasted almonds
Prepare the basic recipe, using 2 ripe mangoes (peeled and pitted) in place of the papayas.

### blueberry & papaya salad with toasted macadamia nuts
Prepare the basic recipe, using macadamia nuts in place of the almonds.

### strawberry & mango salad with toasted almonds
Prepare the basic recipe, using strawberries in place of the blueberries and 2 mangoes (peeled and pitted) in place of the papayas.

# fruit salad with coconut milk

see base recipe page 266

### coconut-topped fruit salad
Prepare the basic recipe, scattering a small handful of toasted coconut flakes over the top of the salad.

### spiced fruit salad with coconut milk
Prepare the basic recipe, omitting the cilantro. Instead, stir 1/4 teaspoon ground cinnamon into the coconut mixture.

### orange, pineapple & banana salad with coconut milk
Prepare the basic recipe, omitting the apple, kiwifruit, and cilantro. Instead, use 1 extra blood orange and 1 extra banana.

### coconut fruit salad with star fruit
Prepare the basic recipe, omitting the apple and cilantro. Instead, add 2 sliced star fruits in place of the apple.

# fig & nectarine salad

see base recipe page 268

### fig & peach salad
Prepare the basic recipe, using 6 peeled, pitted peaches in place of the nectarines.

### fig & nectarine salad with dates
Prepare the basic recipe, scattering 4 chopped, pitted dates over the salad.

### fig & nectarine salad with pistachio nuts
Prepare the basic recipe, sprinkling 2 tablespoons chopped pistachio nuts over the salad.

### fig & plum salad
Prepare the basic recipe, using 8 plums in place of the nectarines.

### nectarine & plum salad with ginger
Prepare the basic recipe, omitting the honey. Instead, add 1 chopped piece stem ginger and 1 tablespoon syrup from the jar.

### fig & nectarine salad with grand marnier
Prepare the basic recipe, using Grand Marnier in place of the rum.

variations

# poached fruit compôte

see base recipe page 270

### poached fruit compôte with dried apricots
Prepare the basic recipe, using 8 dried apricots with the pears.

### poached fruit compôte with figs
Prepare the basic recipe, using 8 halved figs in place of the peaches.

### poached fruit compôte with plums
Prepare the basic recipe, using 8 halved, pitted plums in place of
the peaches.

### poached fruit compôte with slivered almonds
Prepare the basic recipe, scattering 2 tablespoons slivered almonds over
the compôte in place of the nut brittle.

### poached fruit compôte with star anise
Prepare the basic recipe, using star anise in place of the cinnamon stick.

variations

# creamy rice pudding fruit salad

see base recipe page 272

### banana & peach salad with rice pudding
Prepare the basic recipe, replacing the kiwifruit and raspberries with
3 sliced bananas.

### fresh berry salad with rice pudding
Prepare the basic recipe, replacing the kiwifruit and peaches with 1 cup
strawberries (halved or quartered if large) and 1/2 cup blueberries.

### fresh berry & peach salad with rice pudding
Prepare the basic recipe, using 1 cup blueberries in place of the kiwifruit.

### spiced rice pudding & fresh fruit salad
Prepare the basic recipe, adding 1 cinnamon stick to the milk and rice. Remove
from the rice pudding before cooling.

# index